AGES
7 to 11

SCHO

KV-513-435

CHECK FOR CD-ROM

everyday
French

Célébrons
les fêtes

IMPORTANT – Permitted use and warnings

Jan Lewandowski
& Jessica Norrie

Credits and acknowledgements

Minimum specification

PC or Mac with CD-ROM drive and 512 Mb RAM (recommended)
Windows 2000 or above/Mac OSX 10.4
Recommended minimum processor speed: 1.3 Ghz

Acknowledgements

The publishers gratefully acknowledge permission to reproduce the following copyright material: GeoBeats Inc for the use of the film clip 'La crêperie' from www.geobeats.com © 2007, GeoBeats Inc (2007, www.geobeats.com).
© Crown copyright material. Reproduced under the terms of the Click Use Licence.

Every effort has been made to trace copyright holders for the works reproduced in this book, and the publishers apologise for any inadvertent omissions.

Due to the nature of the web, we cannot guarantee the content or links of any website mentioned. We strongly recommend that teachers check websites before using them in the classroom.

Authors
Jan Lewandowski & Jessica Norrie

Commissioning Editor
Juliet Gladston

Development Editors
Kate Pedlar, Niamh O'Carroll & Fabia Lewis

Project Editor
Gina Thorsby

Editor
Tracy Kewley

Series Designers and Cover Artwork
Joy Monkhouse & Sonja Bagley

Illustrations
Moreno Chiacchiera & Jackie Stafford/Beehive Illustration

Designer
Sonja Bagley

CD-ROM design and development team
Joy Monkhouse, Allison Parry, Andrea Lewis, Anna Oliwa & Haremi

Designed using Adobe Indesign
Published by Scholastic Ltd
Book End
Range Road
Witney
Oxfordshire OX29 0YD
Printed by Bell & Bain Ltd, Glasgow
Text © 2010, Jan Lewandowski & Jessica Norrie
© 2010, Scholastic Ltd

1 2 3 4 5 6 7 8 9 0   0 1 2 3 4 5 6 7 8 9

British Library Cataloguing-in-Publication Data
A catalogue record for this book is available from the British Library.
ISBN 978-1407-10208-5

Contents

Resources on the CD-ROM

 Unit 1
Interactive flashcard: *Rama et Sita*
Interactive activity: *Les fêtes de l'île Maurice*
Photocopiable: *Le conte de Rama et Sita*
Translation: *Le conte de Rama et Sita*
Images: *Rama, Sita, Ravana* and *Hanouman*

 Unit 2
Interactive flashcard: *Hanoucca*
Interactive activity: *Les nuits de Hanoucca*
Photocopiable: *Les nuits de Hanoucca*
Photocopiable: *La Ménorah de Hanoucca*

Unit 3
Interactive flashcard: *Les santons*
Interactive activity: *Allons fabriquer les santons !*
Photocopiable: *Allons fabriquer les santons !*

 Unit 4
Interactive flashcard: *Une galette des Rois et des fèves*
Interactive activity: *Les formes*
Photocopiable: *La fête des Rois*
Film: *La fête des Rois*
Film transcript: *La fête des Rois*

 Unit 5
Interactive flashcard: *Les animaux de l'horoscope chinois*
Interactive activity: *Une lanterne chinoise*

 Unit 6
Interactive flashcard: *Les ustensiles*
Interactive activity: *Les ingrédients*
Photocopiable: *La pâte à crêpes*
Photocopiable: *Sois un détective de langue !*
Image: *Carnaval de Bailleul*
Film: *La crêperie*

 Unit 7
Interactive flashcard: *La chasse à l'œuf*
Interactive activity: *La chasse à l'œuf*
Photocopiable: *Mendiants au chocolat*

 Unit 8
Interactive flashcard: *Poisson d'avril*
Interactive activity: *Quel temps fait-il aujourd'hui ?*
Photocopiable: *Quel temps fait-il aujourd'hui ?*
Image: *Muguet du bois*

 Unit 9
Interactive flashcard: *La Fête Nationale*
Interactive activity: *Dictée illustrée*
Photocopiable: *Dictée illustrée*
Photograph: *La Rue Montorgueil*

 Unit 10
Interactive flashcard: *Une mosquée*
Interactive activity: *Les impératifs*
Photocopiable: *Connaissances de base*
Photocopiable: *Une carte d'Aïd*
Translation: *Une carte d'Aïd*

 Unit 11
Interactive flashcard: *Les mois de l'année*
Interactive activity: *Quelle est la date de ton anniversaire ?*
Photocopiable: *Les mois et les nombres*
Photocopiable: *Quelle est la date de ton anniversaire ?*
Song: *Quelle est la date de ton anniversaire ?*
Translation: *Quelle est la date de ton anniversaire ?*

 Unit 12
Interactive flashcard: *Le groupe rock*
Interactive activity: *Les instruments musicaux*
Photocopiable: *Gugusse*
Song: *Gugusse*
Translation: *Gugusse*

Introduction

Introduction

The activities in this book are intended to be practical and enjoyable while at the same time laying some sound foundations for language learning. Most of the units can be taught independently of the others, while others build on previous units.

On pages 8–9 there is a grid linking the units to the KS2 Framework for Languages indicating the relevant strand and, where appropriate, objective, and using the usual abbreviations:

O = Oracy
L = Literacy
IU = Intercultural understanding
LLS = Language learning strategies
KAL = Knowledge about Language

Introducing new core vocabulary

- Always make sure the children are watching and listening. Get into a routine of saying *Regardez !* (Watch!) – make a spectacles shape with your fingers or point to your eyes; *Écoutez !* (Listen!) – gesture to your ear;
- Choose the simplest phrases to introduce first – especially if they are 'cognates' (look or sound like their English equivalents). This builds confidence!
- Only teach a few phrases at a time – so, to start with, try, for example *en autobus* then *en train* and *en bateau*. Play a couple of simple games (see below) then introduce the others.
- Point to/hold up the flashcard as you say the phrase.
- Use gestures to reinforce the meaning – arms stretched out sideways for *en avion* (by plane); hands making 'turning wheel' movements for *en train* (by train) etc.

Games for practising vocabulary

- **Répétez si c'est vrai** – Hold up a flashcard or object and say a word or phrase. The children repeat only if what the teacher says matches the picture or object she is holding.
- **Secret signal** – Sit the children in a horseshoe shape so that they can see each other. Display all the vocabulary items learned in a clear 'list' form. Choose one child to be the 'detective' who will go outside the room (accompanied by a TA perhaps). Choose another child to be the 'secret signaller'. Explain to the children that you are all going to chant the words/ phrases, starting with the one at the beginning of the list. When the secret signaller makes the secret signal (for example rubbing the forehead or scratching an ear) you will all start chanting the next phrase in the list. The aim of the game is for the secret signaller to avoid detection and for the class to chant the phrases for as long as possible.

Introduction

- **Quick whizz** – Put picture cards in a pile with their pictures hidden from the class. Make a play of 'shuffling' the cards. Ask the children to say the word or phrase together when they can see what it is. Take the top one and quickly 'whizz' it, picture facing the children, but making it disappear again very quickly. Repeat as many times as you wish. Keep shuffling and emphasising that it's a game. From the teacher's point of view, this game is about getting the children to practise words and phrases; for the children it's about being the fastest and most observant.

- **Fly swat** – You need two plastic fly-swats and a set of flashcards fixed to a wall or board with sticky putty. The class is divided into two teams and children take turns to come forward. The teacher calls out a phrase/word. The first person to swat the correct flashcard wins a point for his/her team.

- **Salade de fruits** – The purpose of this game is to get children listening (and responding) to language. The children sit on the floor in a circle. Choose a limited number of vocabulary items. Give each child a word/phrase to remember, so that several children have the same phrase. When the teacher calls out one of the words or phrases the children with that phrase must stand up and change places. Now and then, call out *salade de fruits* and all must change places.

- **Hot/cold** – This game is excellent for whole-class practice of a 'hard to pronounce' word or phrase, such as *Qu'est-ce que tu as dans ta chambre ?* (What do you have in your bedroom). The seeker is sent out of the room, while the teacher or child hides the object or flashcard. As the seeker re-enters the room, the class begins to chant the word or phrase repeatedly and rhythmically, getting louder as they get closer, or softer as they move further away, until the object is found.

- **Morpion** (noughts and crosses) – On your class whiteboard, or using an interactive whiteboard, draw a 3 x 3 grid. Stick a word card in each of the squares so that the children can identify their chosen square. Divide the class into two teams – *les cercles* (o) *et les croix* (x). Tell the class: *choisissez une case* (choose a square). Teams take turns to choose a square and a member of the team must say the word on that flashcard to place their nought or cross on the board.

Introducing the written word

- Make reading cards for new words and phrases, so that you can introduce the written form of the new language you have taught in a planned and systematic way.
- When you show the children new word cards, always get them to read them aloud with you, insisting on correct pronunciation.
- Ask the children to tell you about 'surprises' in the spellings (eg silent *s* or *t* at the ends of words).
- Encourage the children to look out for rhymes and patterns, pointing out which vowels make which sounds in French. (eg the letter *i* in *petit*, *il*, *avril* making a sound like the English 'ee').

The gender of nouns

- You may find it helpful to add a system of colour-coding to the word and picture cards (say, red for feminine, blue for masculine) to help children remember which words are masculine and which words are feminine.
- Always introduce nouns with a definite/indefinite article (eg *le parc*, *un lion*) never the noun on its own. This will help children to remember the gender of the noun.

How to use the CD-ROM

Here are brief guidance notes for using the CD-ROM. For more detailed information, see **How to use** on the start-up screen, or **Help** on the relevant screen for information about a particular resource. The CD-ROM follows the structure of the book and contains:

- 12 on-screen interactive activities
- 12 on-screen interactive flashcards
- Audio songs
- Film clips
- Images and poster pages
- All of the photocopiable pages including the song lyrics and English translations

Getting started

To begin using the CD-ROM, simply place it in your CD- or DVD-ROM drive. Although the CD-ROM should auto run, if it fails to do so, navigate to the drive and double click on the red **Start** icon.

Start-up screen

The start-up screen is the first screen that appears. Here you can access: how to use the CD-ROM, terms and conditions, credits and registration links. If you agree to the terms and conditions, click **Start** to continue.

Main menu

The main menu provides links to all of the Units. Clicking on the relevant Unit icon will take you to the Unit screen where you can access all the Unit's resources. Clicking on **Resource finder** will take you to a search screen for all the resources, where you can search by key word or Unit for a specific resource.

Resource finder

The **Resource finder** lists all of the resources on the CD-ROM. You can:

- Select a Unit by choosing the appropriate title from the drop-down menu.
- Search for key words by typing them into the search box.
- Scroll up or down the list of resources to locate the required resource.
- Launch a resource by clicking once on its row on the screen.

- Access the glossary of French words and English translations. (See more information below.)

Navigation

The resources all open in separate windows on top of the menu screen. To close a resource, click on the arrow in the top right-hand corner of the screen. To return to the menu screen you can either close or minimise a resource.

Closing a resource will not close the program. However, if you are in a menu screen, then clicking on the **x** in the top right-hand corner of the screen will close the program. To return to a previous menu screen, you need to click on the **Back** arrow button.

Glossary

All of the interactive activities and interactive flashcards link to a glossary. The glossary will open in a separate window. Simply click first on the desired headletter and then on the French word to reveal the English translation. You can also click on the audio buttons to hear the pronunciation of each French word.

Whiteboard tools

The CD-ROM comes with its own set of whiteboard tools for use on any whiteboard. These include:

- Pen tool
- Highlighter tool
- Eraser
- Sticky note.

Click on the **Tools** button on the right-hand side of the screen to access these tools.

Printing

Print the resources by clicking on the **Print** button. The photocopiable pages print as full A4 portrait pages, but please note if you have a landscape photocopiable page or poster you need to set the orientation to landscape in your print preferences. Printouts of the interactive activities will include what is on the screen. For a full A4 printout you need to set the orientation to landscape in your print preferences.

Framework links

Unit	Oracy	Literacy	Knowledge about language	IU	Language and learning strategies
1	3.1, 3.3 4.1, 4.4 5.1, 5.4 6.2, 6.4	3.1, 3.3 4.2, 4.4 5.1, 5.2, 5.3 6.4	**Year 3:** Imitate pronunciation of sounds; recognise how sounds are represented in written form. **Year 4:** Use question forms. **Year 5:** Recognise patterns in simple sentences; manipulate language by changing an element in a sentence; apply knowledge of rules when building sentences; develop accuracy in pronunciation. **Year 6:** Use knowledge of words, text and structure to build simple spoken and written passages.	3.2, 3.4 4.1, 4.3 5.1, 5.2 6.2, 6.3	• Write new words. • Read and memorise words. • Access information sources. • Integrate new language into previously learned language. • Apply grammatical knowledge to make sentences. • Use context and previous knowledge to help understanding and reading skills.
2	3.4 4.2 5.4 6.3	3.1, 3.3 4.3, 4.4 5.1, 5.2, 5.3 6.1, 6.2	**Year 3:** Imitate pronunciation of sounds; notice the spelling of familiar words. **Year 4:** Reinforce and extend recognition of word classes and understand their function. **Year 5:** Recognise patterns in simple sentences; manipulate language by changing an element in a sentence; apply knowledge of rules when building sentences; recognise the typical conventions of word order in the foreign language; understand that words will not always have a direct equivalent in the language. **Year 6:** Use knowledge of word and text conventions to build sentences and short texts.	3.3, 3.4 4.1 5.2, 5.3 6.2	• Write new words. • Read and memorise words. • Apply knowledge about simple grammatical forms to experiment with writing. • Access information sources. • Apply grammatical knowledge to make sentences. • Integrate new languages into previously learned language. • Use a word list. • Apply a range of linguistic knowledge to create simple written production. • Make predictions based on existing knowledge.
3	3.2, 3.3, 3.4 4.2, 4.4 5.1, 5.3, 5.4 6.3, 6.4	3.1 4.1, 4.3 5.2 6.1	**Year 3:** Imitate pronunciation of sounds; recognise question forms and negatives. **Year 4:** Reinforce and extend recognition of word classes and understand their function. **Year 5:** Recognise patterns in simple sentences; manipulate language by changing an element in a sentence; apply knowledge of rules when building sentences. **Year 6:** Discuss language learning and reflect and share ideas and experiences; use knowledge of words, text and structure to build simple spoken and written passages.	3.3 4.1 5.1 6.2	• Practise new language with a friend. • Use context and previous knowledge to determine meaning and pronunciation. • Read and memorise words. • Plan and prepare – analyse what needs to be done to carry out a task. • Apply grammatical knowledge to make sentences.
4	3.2, 3.3, 3.4 4.2, 4.4 5.1, 5.3, 5.4 6.3, 6.4	3.1 4.1, 4.3 5.2 6.1	**Year 3:** Identify specific sounds, phonemes and words; imitate pronunciation of sounds; hear main word classes. **Year 4:** Recognise and extend knowledge of word classes and understand their function; apply phonic knowledge of the language to support reading and writing. **Year 5:** Recognise patterns in simple sentences. **Year 6:** Recognise patterns in the foreign language; use knowledge of words, text and structure to build simple spoken and written passages.	3.3, 3.4 4.1 5.1, 5.3 6.1	• Use actions and rhymes to aid memorisation. • Use the context of what they see/hear and previous knowledge to determine some of the meaning. • Read and memorise words. • Integrate new language into previously learned language. • Listen for clues to meaning eg tone of voice, key words. • Make predictions based on previous knowledge.
5	3.2, 3.3, 3.4 4.2, 4.3 5.3 6.1, 6.3	3.1, 3.2 4.1, 4.3 5.2 6.2	**Year 3:** Identify specific sounds, phonemes and words; imitate pronunciation of sounds; hear main word classes; recognise how sounds are represented in written form. **Year 4:** Reinforce and extend recognition of word classes and understand their function; apply simple agreements, singular and plural. **Year 5:** Recognise patterns in simple sentences; recognise the typical conventions of word order in the foreign language. **Year 6:** Recognise patterns in the foreign language; use knowledge of word and text conventions to build sentences and short texts.	3.3 4.1 5.3 6.2	• Play games to aid memorisation. • Use the context of what they see/hear to determine some of the meaning. • Compare the language with English. • Plan and prepare for a language activity. • Read and memorise words. • Access information sources. • Use context and previous knowledge to help understanding. • Look and listen for visual and aural clues. • Listen for clues to meaning eg tone of voice, key words.
6	3.2, 3.4 4.2 5.3 6.3	3.1, 3.2 4.1, 4.2, 4.3 5.1 6.1	**Year 3:** Identify specific sounds, phonemes and words; imitate pronunciation of sounds; notice the spelling of familiar words; recognise that languages describe familiar things differently. **Year 4:** Recognise that texts in different languages will often have the same conventions of style and layout; apply phonic knowledge of the language to support reading and writing. **Year 5:** Recognise patterns in simple sentences; recognise the typical conventions of word order in the foreign language; understand that words will not always have a direct equivalent in the language. **Year 6:** Recognise patterns in the foreign language; use knowledge of word and text conventions to build sentences and short texts.	3.2, 3.3, 3.4 4.1, 4.2 5.1, 5.3 6.2	• Use the context of what they see/hear to determine some of the meaning. • Compare the language with English. • Use context and previous knowledge to determine meaning and pronunciation. • Plan and prepare for a language activity. • Read and memorise words. • Access information sources. • Look and listen for visual and aural clues.

Unit	Oracy	Literacy	Knowledge about language	IU	Language and learning strategies
7	3.1, 3.3, 3.4 4.1, 4.2, 4.4 5.1, 5.4 6.1	3.1 4.4 5.2 6.1, 6.3	**Year 3:** Identify specific sounds, phonemes and words; imitate pronunciation of sounds. **Year 4:** Reinforce and extend recognition of word classes and understand their function; recognise and apply simple agreements, singular and plural. **Year 5:** Recognise patterns in simple sentences; manipulate language by changing an element in a sentence; apply knowledge of rules when building sentences; develop accuracy in pronunciation; understand that words will not always have a direct equivalent in the language. **Year 6:** Recognise patterns in the foreign language; notice and match agreements; use knowledge of word order and sentence construction to support the understanding of the written text.	3.3 4.1, 4.2 5.3 6.3	• Use actions and rhymes and play games to aid memorisation. • Practise new language with a friend. • Read and memorise words. • Use context and previous knowledge to help understanding. • Look and listen for visual and aural clues.
8	3.1, 3.2, 3.3, 3.4 4.1, 4.2, 4.3 5.1, 5.2 6.1, 6.4	3.1, 3.3 4.1, 4.3, 4.4 5.1, 5.2, 5.3 6.3, 6.4	**Year 3:** Identify specific sounds, phonemes and words; imitate pronunciation of sounds; recognise question forms and negatives. **Year 4:** Use question forms; apply phonic knowledge of the language to support reading and writing. **Year 5:** Recognise patterns in simple sentences; develop accuracy in pronunciation and intonation; recognise the typical conventions of word order in the foreign language. **Year 6:** Recognise patterns in the foreign language; notice and match agreements; use knowledge of word and text conventions to build sentences and short texts.	3.3 4.1, 4.2 5.1, 5.3 6.2	• Use actions and rhymes and play games to aid memorisation. • Practise new language with a friend. • Read and memorise words. • Write new words. • Compare the language with English. • Use context and previous knowledge to aid understanding. • Apply a range of linguistic knowledge to create simple, written production.
9	3.1, 3.2, 3.3, 3.4 4.2, 4.3 5.3 6.1, 6.3	3.2, 3.3 4.1, 4.2, 4.3 5.2, 5.3 6.3	**Year 3:** Identify specific sounds, phonemes and words; imitate pronunciation of sounds; recognise how sounds are represented in written form. **Year 4:** Apply phonic knowledge of the language to support reading and writing. **Year 5:** Recognise patterns in simple sentences; develop accuracy in pronunciation and intonation; understand that words will not always have a direct equivalent in the language. **Year 6:** Recognise patterns in the foreign language; use knowledge of word and text conventions to build sentences and short texts.	3.3, 3.4 4.1, 4.2 5.2, 5.3 6.2, 6.3	• Use actions and rhymes and play games to aid memorisation. • Look at the face of the person speaking and listen attentively. • Compare the language with English. • Read and memorise words. • Access information sources. • Look and listen for visual and aural clues.
10	3.3, 3.4 4.2, 4.3 5.1, 5.3 6.1, 6.2	3.1, 3.2 4.1, 4.3 5.2 6.1, 6.3	**Year 3:** Identify specific sounds, phonemes and words; imitate pronunciation of sounds; recognise how sounds are represented in written form. **Year 4:** Use question forms; reinforce and extend recognition of word classes and understand their function; recognise the typical conventions of word order in the foreign language. **Year 5:** Recognise patterns in simple sentences; develop accuracy in pronunciation. **Year 6:** Recognise patterns in the foreign language; notice and match agreements.	3.2, 3.4 4.1, 4.4 5.2 6.3	• Practise new language with a friend. • Look at the face of the person speaking and listen attentively. • Compare the language with English. • Read and memorise words. • Access information sources.
11	3.1, 3.2, 3.3 4.1, 4.4 5.1 6.4	3.2 4.1, 4.3, 4.4 5.2, 5.3 6.3	**Year 3:** Identify specific sounds, phonemes and words; imitate pronunciation of sounds; hear main word classes; recognise question forms and negatives; recognise that languages describe things differently. **Year 4:** Recognise and apply simple agreements, singular and plural; use question forms. **Year 5:** Apply knowledge of rules when building sentences; appreciate that different languages use different writing conventions. **Year 6:** Recognise patterns in the foreign language; notice and match agreements.	4.1, 4.3	• Practise new language with a friend. • Compare the language with English. • Read and memorise words. • Sort words into categories. • Apply grammatical knowledge to make sentences.
12	3.1, 3.3 4.2 5.4 6.2	4.3 5.2 6.2	**Year 3:** Imitate pronunciation of sounds; recognise how sounds are represented in written form. **Year 4:** Reinforce and extend recognition of word classes and understand their function. **Year 5:** Recognise patterns in simple sentences; manipulate language by changing an element in a sentence; apply knowledge of rules when building sentences; develop accuracy in pronunciation; understand that words will not always have a direct equivalent in the language. **Year 6:** Recognise patterns in the foreign language; notice and match agreements.	3.3 4.2 5.1, 5.3 6.3	• Use actions and rhymes to aid memorisation. • Compare the language with English. • Plan and prepare for a language activity. • Access information sources. • Apply grammatical knowledge to make sentences. • Look and listen for visual/aural clues. • Use a word list. • Apply a range of linguistic knowledge to create simple written production.

Unit 1: Diwali

Objective

To learn the French required to retell the Diwali story.

Introducing the vocabulary

- Explain to the children that there are many French-speaking Hindus around the world. There are approximately 121,000 Hindus in France itself, but there are many more French-speaking Hindus outside France, in places such as La Réunion, Mauritius, Guadeloupe and French Guinea.
- Explain that Diwali is an important Hindu festival and use 'Interactive flashcard: *Rama et Sita*' from the CD-ROM to introduce the main characters in the story of Rama and Sita. (Recap the story if necessary.) Ask the question on the flashcard *Qui es-tu ?* and let the children practise answering using *Je suis ...*

Vocabulary extension

- For older children introduce the third person: *Qui est-ce ?* (Who is it?) *C'est ...* (It's...).
- The activity could be extended by adding negatives. Give out the four images of *Rama, Sita, Ravana* and *Hanouman* from the CD-ROM, face down to four children. Allow the children to look at their pictures, and the rest of the class to guess the character, for example: *Tu es Rama ? Non, je ne suis pas Rama*, or *C'est Rama ? Non, ce n'est pas Rama.*

Core activities

- Explain to the children that they are going to perform the story of Rama and Sita in French.
- Ask the children to draw large labelled pictures of *un palais*, *une forêt*, *une île*, *une ville*. These will be used to introduce the four scenes to the audience.
- Allocate the parts listed on photocopiable page 34 (*Le conte de Rama et Sita*). Have groups of children for the ten-headed monster, the monkey army, the demon army and the narrators. (A translation of the play is available on the CD-ROM.)
- Use the script to perform the story.

Extension activities

- Locate Mauritius on a world map.
- Explain that there are many different religions practised in Mauritius. Use 'Interactive activity: *Les fêtes de l'île Maurice*' to find out about some of the holidays celebrated in Mauritius. The children are required to match the holiday to the reason for it.

Resources

Interactive flashcard: *Rama et Sita*

Interactive activity: *Les fêtes de l'île Maurice*

Photocopiable page 34: *Le conte de Rama et Sita*

Translation: *Le conte de Rama et Sita*

Images: *Rama, Sita, Ravana* and *Hanouman*

Preparation

A version of the story of Rama and Sita (optional)

Props for the story of Rama and Sita: items to represent the palace, forest; bridge; bow and arrows; ten ugly masks for the monster; monkey masks (easy to make from paper plates on lolly sticks); divas; crowns

Interactive whiteboard

List of bank holidays in Mauritius		
Date	**Name of holiday**	**Reason for holiday**
le 1er janvier	*Le jour de l' an*	*Jour férié*
le 2 janvier	*Le lendemain du jour de l'an*	*Jour férié*
le 1er février	*Le jour de l'abolition de l'esclavage*	*Fête historique*
le 12 mars	*Le jour de l'indépendance*	*Fête nationale*
le 1er mai	*Le jour du travail*	*Jour férié*
le 15 août	*L'Assomption*	*Fête catholique*
le 1er novembre	*La Toussaint*	*Fête catholique*
le 25 décembre	*Le jour de Noël*	*Fête catholique*
mi janvier/début février	*Le Thaipoosam Cavadee*	*Fête tamoule*
fin janvier/début février	*Le jour de l'an chinois*	*Fête bouddhiste*
février/mars	*Maha Shivaratree*	*Fête hindoue*
mars	*Ougadi*	*Fête hindoue*
août/septembre	*Ganesh Chaturthi*	*Fête hindoue*
octobre/novembre	*Diwali ou le Dipavali*	*Fête hindoue*
les dates varient chaque année	*Aïd al-Fitr*	*Fête musulmane marquant la fin du mois de ramadan – mois de jeûne*

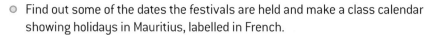

○ Find out some of the dates the festivals are held and make a class calendar showing holidays in Mauritius, labelled in French.

Cross-curricular ideas

Geography: To locate Mauritius on a map and find out about religious buildings.

Find out about the history of Mauritius using books and the internet. Find pictures of different religious buildings on the island so that you can illustrate the class calendar.

Maths: To represent data as a bar graph.

Make a bar graph to show how the bank holidays represent religions in Mauritius.

Five-minute follow-ups

○ Ask groups to come up with extra dialogue for the Rama and Sita play, for example *j'ai peur, j'ai faim*.

○ Look at the website of the Tamil temple in Paris, France, at **www.templeganesh.fr**

○ Research one of the other Hindu festivals celebrated in Mauritius.

Key words

Core:

Hindou/Hindoue – Hindu (noun)

hindou/hindoue – Hindu (adjective)

le (vieux*) roi – the (old) king

la (vieille*) reine – the (old) queen

le prince Rama – Prince Rama

la princesse Sita – Princess Sita

le vieillard – the old man

Hanouman, le dieu-singe – Hanuman the monkey god

Ravana, le monstre à dix têtes – Ravana, the ten-headed monster

l'armée (f) *des singes* – the monkey army

Extension:

un temple – temple

l'île Maurice – Mauritius

Key phrases

Core:

le conte de Rama et Sita – the story of Rama and Sita

Je suis ... – I am...

Nous sommes ... – We are...

Extension:

Où est l'île Maurice ? – Where is Mauritius?

les jours fériés (m) – (bank) holidays

les fêtes religieuses (f) – religious festivals

les fêtes culturelles (f) – cultural festivals

Trouvez les fêtes hindoues – Find the Hindu festivals

(C'est au) début février – (It's at the) beginning of February

(C'est en) mi février – (It's) mid February

(C'est à la) fin février – (It's at the) end of February

l'abolition (f) *de l'esclavage* (m) – the abolition of slavery

Quelle est la date de la fête de ... ? – What is the date of the festival of...?

Language points

Telling the story will provide practice with the first person singular and plural present tense *je .../nous ...*

Words for the different religions when used as an adjective (*une fête hindoue/un temple hindou*) do not have capital letters.

Month names are not capitalised either: *La fête de ... est au mois de mai*.

* Differentiation is possible here by adding or omitting the agreeing adjectives, depending on the level of the group.

Unit 2: Voilà la lumière !

Objectives

To know French words and phrases associated with two festivals of light; to learn ordinal numbers.

Introducing the vocabulary

- Tell the children about the eight days of Hanukkah when Jewish people light a menorah to remember their victory 2000 years ago over the Syrian-Greek king, Antiochus, who had banned them from praying. When they reclaimed their temple, they found everything broken and dirty. They had very little oil to keep the temple lamp lit but miraculously just enough oil appeared for eight nights until the temple was clean and the usual supply of oil was restored.
- Use 'Interactive flashcard: *Hanoucca*' to introduce the vocabulary for the objects relating to Hanukkah. Ask: *Qu'est-ce que c'est ?* (What is it?) Encourage the children to reply in sentences, for example: *C'est une bougie*.
- Introduce the words 'first', 'next', 'then', 'after', and 'last' as well as the ordinal numbers. Display 'Photocopiable: *Les nuits de Hanoucca*' from the CD-ROM; use 'Interactive activity: *Les nuits de Hanoucca*' to reinforce some of the vocabulary. Double click on the phrases to hear them spoken.

Resources

Interactive flashcard: *Hanoucca*

Interactive activity: *Les nuits de Hanoucca*

Photocopiable: *Les nuits de Hanoucca*

Photocopiable page 35: *La Ménorah de Hanoucca*

Preparation

To make the menorah: poster-sized blue paper; contrasting card (for candles and shamash/ servant candle); gold paper scraps (for flames); Blu-tack®

Core activities

- Explain to the children that there are approximately 491,000 Jewish people in France, nearly four per cent of the population, and about 4,000 in Morocco and Tunisia where French is widely spoken.
- Tell the children that they are going to make a display of the menorah and label it with repeating phrases to show the special way it is lit during Hanukkah.
- Display the menorah shape from photocopiable page 35 (*La Ménorah de Hanoucca*). Refer back to the interactive activity about lighting the menorah to show the children how each of the candles will eventually be placed and lit. (Note: candles are placed from right to left and lit from left to right.)
- Over eight days, 'light' each candle by sticking on the paper flames as well as the appropriate text from 'Photocopiable: *Les nuits de Hanoucca*' using Blu-tack®. Ask the children which words they think they will need to repeat as the instructions get longer – *d'abord, ensuite, puis, après, finalement*. As the days progress, more children will be able to predict and formulate an appropriate phrase for the instructions.

Extension activities

- Find out about other festivals of light such as the one held on 8 December in Lyon. Visit the official website **www.lumieres.lyon.fr/lumieres/sections/fr** for a slideshow of events.
- Celebrate your own class *fête de la lumière*. Ask the children to draw their own pictures of buildings. Mount the pictures with a wide white border. In the border space use colour and arrows to show how to light it for their own *fête de la lumière*. Label the features using the modelled sentences in the extension key phrases. You could also use the Paint programme to do this with ICT.

Cross-curricular ideas

Science: To investigate reversible and non-reversible changes.
For a science link, light candles on a real menorah. They are supposed to burn for half an hour. Weigh the candles before and after and discuss reversible and irreversible changes.

RE: To recognise the important features of menorahs.
Menorahs can have lots of different shapes as long as there is a central holder for the servant candle and a row of eight more for the daily candles. Design your own menorah. Label the picture with the French words for 'candle', 'flame', and the title *Joyeux Hanoucca, la fête de la lumière*.

Five-minute follow-ups

- The dreidel (*la toupie*) is a toy associated with Hanukkah. There are instructions in French on how to make and play with one at www.momes.net/dictionnaire/minidossiers/bricolage/dreidel.html
- Teach the children the French version of the dreidel song:

  Toupie tourne tourne tourne
  Hanoucca est une belle fête
  Hanoucca est une belle fête
  Toupie tourne tourne tourne
  C'est une joyeuse fête pour le peuple
  Un grand miracle est arrivé là-bas
  Un grand miracle est arrivé là-bas
  C'est une joyeuse fête pour le peuple

Key words

Core:

une bougie – a candle
huit jours (m) – eight days
la Ménorah – the menorah
le Chamach – the shamash (servant candle)
le coucher de soleil – the sunset
la flamme – the flame
d'abord – first of all
ensuite – next/after that
après – after
puis – then
finalement – lastly
la fenêtre – the window
la place – the place
(note: this means 'position' and also 'square' as in a town)

Extension:

décembre – December
la lumière – the light
l'ombre (f) – the shadow, shade
l'électricité (f) – electricity
l'arrondissement (m) – the district (of a city)

Key phrases

Core:

Qu'est-ce que c'est? – What is it?
on met ... – one puts (we put)
on allume ... – one lights (we light)
allumez la bougie avec le Chamach – light the candle with the shamash
au centre – in the centre
à droite – to the right
la première nuit – the first night
la deuxième nuit – the second night
la troisième nuit – the third night
la quatrième nuit – the fourth night
la cinquième nuit – the fifth night
la sixième nuit – the sixth night
la septième nuit – the seventh night
la huitième nuit – the eighth night
la dernière nuit – the last night

Extension:

Regardez les illuminations – Look at the illuminations
Regardez les bâtiments – Look at the buildings
Regardez par arrondissement – Look by district
à l'ombre – in the shade/shadow
à la lumière – in the light
La porte est à l'ombre – The door is in the shade
La fenêtre est à la lumière (verte) – The window is in the (green) light
La fontaine est illuminée en blanc – The fountain is illuminated in white
Le bateau est illuminé en bleu – The boat is illuminated in blue

Language points

- The abbreviation for 1st is *1er* or *1ère* depending whether what follows is masculine or feminine (e.g. *le 1er jour* but *la 1ère année*).
- The abbreviations for 2nd, 3rd, 4th etc are the same – *2ème, 3ème, 4ème* and so on. Apart from *1er*, ordinals are not used for months e.g. *le 1er mai*, but it then goes *le 2 mai, le 3 mai* etc. However ordinals are used for districts (*arrondissements*) in cities such as Paris and Lyon.
- The use of *on* translates as 'one' as in 'one eats' but in French it is much more commonly used than in English and is less formal. It is used as a way of describing events, and giving general information without using the passive form. The verb form is the same as for *il/elle*, for example on mange.
- Note: Lyon, like Marseille, has a final 's' in English but not in French.

Unit 3: La fête de Noël dans la région de Provence

Objectives

To learn French words and phrases associated with Christmas; to learn phrases that use the simple future tense.

Introducing the vocabulary

- Explain that Provence is a region of south-east France where the people have their own local traditions, music and art.
- Introduce the word *santons*. Explain that these are tiny hand-painted figures made out of Provençal clay called *argile*. They are displayed in a nativity scene (*une crèche traditionelle*) from early December to mid January. *Les Rois* (the Kings) are not put in place until the feast of the Epiphany on 6 January (see Unit 4).
- Use 'Interactive flashcard: *Les santons*' to identify the main nativity characters and examples of other members of the public who are typically included in nativity scenes.
- Ask *C'est qui ?* (Who is it?) and encourage the children to answer, for example, *C'est un Roi mage* before clicking on the *santon* to check their answer.

Vocabulary extension

- Ask the children to think of other characters that could be made into *santons* and ask each other who they are, for example: *Qui c'est ? C'est le fermier*.

Core activities

- Explain to the children that they are going to make their own *santons*. Talk about the different tasks the children will need to carry out using 'Photocopiable: *Allons fabriquer les santons !*' from the CD-ROM.
- Look at photographs of *santons* on the internet. Go to www.santonsdidier.com (then click on *santons*).
- Use 'Interactive activity: *Allons fabriquer les santons !*' to reinforce the vocabulary. The children match the sentences about making *santons* to the pictures of the tasks.
- The children can then make their *santons* and arrange them in a scene.

Extension activities

- Visit www.santonsmarcelcarbonel.com/glossaire_multilingue for a list of all the *santons* made by this workshop.
- Challenge the children to make up a French dialogue between *santons* and act it out.

Cross-curricular ideas

Geography: To learn the location and some features of Provence.

Find Provence on a map of France. Ask the children if they know what else is associated with this region of France. (You can find information about the region at www.web-provence.com)

ICT: To use a digital camera and combine text with graphics.

Ask the children to take and to save a photograph of the *santons* scene they have made. They can then add speech bubbles and a simple statement for each figure. You can again use the construction *nous allons*:

Nous allons télécharger la photographie – We're going to upload the photo

Nous allons insérer une bulle – We're going to insert a speech bubble

Nous allons insérer une boîte de texte – We're going to insert a text box

Nous allons faire un diaporama – We're going to make a slide show

Art and design: To find out about the works of famous artists.

Gauguin, Van Gogh, Cézanne, Dufy, and Picasso are famous artists who spent time in Provence. Have the children find the pictures of Provence that these artists painted.

Resources

Interactive flashcard: *Les santons*

Interactive activity: *Allons fabriquer les santons !*

Photocopiable: *Allons fabriquer les santons !*

Preparation

Gather materials for making the *santons*: clay (air-hardening modelling clay is easiest to use and doesn't need firing); paint; diluted white glue to glaze (optional)

Interactive whiteboard

Unit 3: La fête de Noël dans
la région de Provence

Tips

Make a nativity scene
from the children's
santons and display
it in the classroom or
hall.

Five-minute follow-ups

- In Provence and elsewhere in France, the traditional Christmas meal has 13 desserts. Can the children find out why, and what they are? (13 represents the number of people at the Last Supper and each dessert has a special meaning.)
- In France, St Nicholas visits homes on 6 December. Children put out a pair of shoes, to be filled with presents. They hope that they won't just get a switch (cane) from St Nicholas' companion, *le Père Fouettard* who visits naughty children. Learn a song about St Nicholas in English or French. Find words and music at **www.momes.net/comtpines/comptines-noel.html**

Key words

Core:

La Provence – Provence
des santons (m) – traditional miniature clay crèche figures from Provence
l'argile (f) – Provençal clay
regarder – to look
peindre – to paint
modeler – to model
poser – to put
demain – tomorrow
après-demain – the day after tomorrow
miniature – miniature
Jésus – Jesus
Marie – Mary
Joseph – Joseph
les Rois (m) *mages* – the three kings
un berger – shepherd

Extension:

un bœuf – an ox
un mouton – a sheep
un agneau – a lamb
un chameau – a camel
un âne – a donkey

Key phrases

Core:

Nous allons voir une crèche traditionelle – We are going to see a traditional nativity crib
Nous allons fabriquer/modeler/ peindre/poser/photographier les santons – We are going to make/ model/paint/position/photograph the *santons*
C'est qui ? – Who is it?
C'est Marie – It is Mary
C'est la mère de Jésus – She is Jesus' mother
C'est un Roi mage – It's a king
C'est un berger – It's a shepherd
C'est une femme aux fleurs – It's a woman with flowers

Extension:

C'est un boulanger – It's a baker
C'est une femme à la courge – It's a woman with a gourd
C'est un homme aux fruits – It's a man with fruit
Posez les santons en groupes – Put the *santons* in groups.
Regardez les animaux de la crèche – Look at the animals in the nativity scene
Je suis Marie, la mère de Jésus – I am Mary, mother of Jesus
Je suis un Roi ; j'offre de l'or – I am a king; I am giving gold
Je suis un berger ; j'offre un agneau – I am a shepherd; I am giving a lamb
Je suis une femme provençale ; j'offre des fleurs – I am a Provençal woman; I am giving flowers

Language points

- The word *santons* comes from the Provençal language, meaning 'little saint'. Although *santons* include the Holy Family and other traditional figures of the Nativity, there are also many ordinary people and animals, for example the lemon seller, the chestnut seller.
- A simple future tense can be made using the present tense of the verb *aller* (to go) plus an infinitive; thus *nous allons* + infinitive means 'we are going to (do)...'.

Unit 4: La fête des Rois

Objectives

To learn French words and phrases related to *la fête des Rois*; to learn French words for shapes.

Introducing the vocabulary

- Show the children 'Film: *La fête des Rois*' and ask them in English what they think the family is doing. Why they think the people might be eating a special cake? How can they tell it is a special occasion? (They are drinking champagne; the boy is wearing a crown.) Can the children suggest what the occasion might be?
- Use 'Interactive flashcard: *Une galette des Rois et des fèves*' to introduce the core vocabulary.

Core activities

- Show the film clip again. Explain that this celebration takes place shortly after Christmas. If the children suggest New Year explain that the French do celebrate New Year, and that they tend to send New Year cards rather than Christmas cards. People wish each other *Bonne Année*. Is this what the people in the video are saying? (No.)
- Explain that this is a festival which takes place in France and in some other francophone countries on 6 January. It is called *la fête des Rois* and commemorates the Three Kings (or Three Wise Men) finding the baby Jesus in Bethlehem. As part of the festival people eat a special cake called *la galette des Rois*.
- If anyone notices that these older children are drinking wine, explain that France is a wine-growing country and it is the custom for children to drink a very small amount of wine on special occasions. The wine is often mixed with water for children.
- Give the children photocopiable page 36 (*La fête des Rois*) which explains what is happening in the film clip. Read through the text together. Ask the children if they can guess the meaning of the highlighted words. Ask the children to answer the questions and then go through their answers with them. How did they work out the translation (looking for cognates etc)?
- Explain that in days gone by the *fève* was a dried broad bean. The modern *fèves* are usually small porcelain figures, not just nativity figures but also cartoon characters and even football players, as in the film.

Extension activities

- Make crowns with the children. Using a piece of string, ask the children to measure the circumference of their heads (*la circonférence de la tête*) to give them the sizes of their crowns; add an extra five centimetres for overlap.
- Let the children design and cut out their crowns. Before joining the ends together, they should add the gummed paper shapes as jewels (*des bijoux*). Go through the 2D shape names beforehand using 'Interactive activity: *Les formes*'. Double click on the shape names to hear them spoken.

Cross-curricular ideas

D&T: To use a range of skills and techniques to make a *galette des Rois*.
Make a *galette des Rois* for the children to share and taste. You will find many recipes on the internet by searching for *recette galette des Rois*. Stewed apple can be substituted for the marzipan paste in case of a nut allergy. A jelly baby could be inserted into one or more slices just before serving as a 'safe' substitute for a *fève*!

RE/PSHE: To compare a festival in the UK with a festival in France.
Ask the children to find out the name for 6 January in the UK (Epiphany). Ask: *what happens in the UK on this day?* (We take down our Christmas decorations.) Find out the reasons for this.

Resources

Interactive flashcard:
Une galette des Rois et des fèves

Interactive activity:
Les formes

Photocopiable page 36:
La fête des Rois

Film: *La fête des Rois*

Film transcript:
La fête des Rois

Preparation

Materials to make a crown: silver or gold card or paper; coloured gummed geometric shapes; lengths of string; rulers; stapler

Interactive whiteboard

Tips

La fête des Rois makes an excellent first lesson or assembly at the beginning of the spring term.

Five-minute follow-ups

- Act out the scene from photocopiable page 36 (*La fête des Rois*).
- Learn the traditional song *J'aime la galette*:

J'aime la galette	I love galette,
Savez-vous comment ?	Do you know how much?
Quand elle est bien faite	When it's made well
Avec du beurre dedans	With butter inside!
Tra la la la la la la la lère	Tra la la la la la la la lère
Tra la la la la la la la la	Tra la la la la la la la la
Tra la la la la la la lère	Tra la la la la la la la lère
Tra la la la la la la la la	Tra la la la la la la la la

Key words

Core:

aujourd'hui – today
parce que – because
une fête – a festival or special day
aussi – also
dans – in
il y a – there is, there are
une tranche – a slice
une couronne – a crown
une fève – a charm (hidden in cake for *la fête des Rois*)
sous – under
la table – the table
une fourchette – a fork
une assiette – a plate
un verre à vin – a wine glass

Extension:

le papier/le carton – the paper/card
des gommettes (f) – gummed paper shapes
des ciseaux (m) – scissors
une ficelle – a length of string
un carré – a square
un triangle – a triangle
un rectangle – a rectangle
un cercle – a circle
un ovale – an oval
un losange – a diamond

Key phrases

Core:

la fête des Rois – the Festival of the Kings
C'est le six janvier – It is the 6th of January
Nous mangeons – We eat
un gâteau spécial – a special cake
Le gâteau s'appelle ... – The cake is called...
la galette des Rois – a *galette des Rois* (no translation – a puff pastry cake filled with marzipan paste)
C'est délicieux – It's delicious
Les parents boivent du champagne – The parents drink champagne
Les enfants boivent un tout petit peu – The children drink a very small amount

pour chaque personne – for each person
(il/elle) porte – (he/she) wears
Il faut trouver la fève – You have to find the *fève*
Il faut finir la galette – You have the finish the cake
Vive le roi ! – Long live the king!
Vive la reine ! – Long live the queen!
le plus petit (enfant) – the smallest (child)
le plus jeune (enfant) – the youngest (child)
un bijou – a jewel
des bijoux (m) – jewels
il/elle choisit – he/she chooses

Extension:

la circonférence de la tête – circumference of the head

Language points

- *Manger* is not a regular 'er' verb ; an 'e' is added in the *nous* form.
- *Il faut* (it is necessary) is usually followed by an infinitive, for example *il faut manger*. It is impersonal but could be translated as 'you have to'.
- *Champagne* with a capital 'C' is the *département*; the drink *champagne* has a lower case 'c'.
- Some nouns are made plural by adding 'x' rather than an 's', for example *bijou, bijoux*. The children may have come across *genoux* (knees).

Unit 5: Le nouvel an chinois

Objectives

To know French words and phrases related to Chinese New Year and to use some of them in different contexts; to know the months of the year.

Introducing the vocabulary

- Explain to the children that, in common with many other countries worldwide, Chinese New Year is celebrated in January/February in Paris and other French-speaking towns and cities.
- According to the Chinese horoscope, each year has an animal symbol (see table opposite). The years rotate on a 12-year cycle starting with the dragon.
- Use 'Interactive flashcard: *Les animaux de l'horoscope chinois*' to introduce the animal names.

Année	Date du nouvel an	Signe
2000	5 février	dragon
2001	24 janvier	serpent
2002	12 février	cheval
2003	1er février	chèvre
2004	22 janvier	singe
2005	9 février	coq
2006	29 janvier	chien
2007	18 février	cochon
2008	7 février	rat
2009	26 janvier	bœuf
2010	14 février	tigre
2011	3 février	lapin

Vocabulary extension

- Tell the children that, according to Chinese tradition, the animal of the year of birth defines our character.
- Invite the children to work out the animal of their birth year. Some children may be able to say it in French, for example *Je suis né(e) en 2000; je suis un dragon*.

Core activities

- Tell the children that you are going to show them how to make a Chinese lantern (*une lanterne chinoise*); these are traditionally used to mark the end of the New Year festivities. Explain that you are going to demonstrate how to make the lantern, speaking in French only.
- Ask some of the children to give out the materials: *distribue/distribuez le papier rouge, les feutres, la colle, les ciseaux*. Show the children all the equipment and let them practise saying the new words.
- Go through the instructions, giving the children time to copy and complete:

1. *Prenez le papier rouge.* (Take the red paper.)
2. *Coupez une bande avec les ciseaux.* (Cut a strip with the scissors.)
3. *Choisissez un animal et dessinez l'animal sur le papier.* (Choose an animal and draw it on the paper.)
4. *Coloriez l'animal avec les feutres.* (Colour in the animal with the felt tips.)
5. *Pliez le papier en deux horizontalement.* (Fold the paper in half horizontally.)
6. *Coupez des lignes verticalement.* (Cut lines vertically.)
7. *Ouvrez le papier.* (Open the paper.)
8. *Formez un tube.* (Form a tube.)
9. *Collez le tube.* (Glue the tube together.)
10. *Attachez la bande avec la colle.* (Glue on the strip (handle).)

Extension activities

- Using 'Interactive activity: *Une lanterne chinoise*', the children can match the instructions to the pictures of lantern-making. Remind them to double click on the instructions to hear them spoken.
- Write two headings on the board: *la jungle* (the jungle) and *la ferme* (the farm). Ask the children to sort the animals into their habitats. They will find that one animal does not fit into either one. Can they suggest a suitable habitat for the dragon? Some children may suggest 'cave'. Note that in French *la cave* is a cellar; *la caverne* or *la grotte* is a cave. Some children may suggest the word 'imaginary'; explain that *imaginaire* is the word they need: *c'est un animal imaginaire*.

Cross-curricular ideas

D&T: To make a Chinese lucky envelope.
It is traditional at Chinese New Year to offer 'lucky' envelopes containing money (chocolate euros or *Bonne année/Bonne chance* greetings could substitute real money). Ask the children to design and make their own envelopes. Have them research the traditional colours (red and gold) and designs for these envelopes.

Science: To find out about different animal habitats.
Ask the children to find out more about the different habitats of the animals from the Chinese horoscope and to create an animal fact file for each one.

Five-minute follow-ups

- Play line bingo using the names of the animals. Each child places five animals in a row. A caller randomly calls out each animal. The players can only turn over the matching animal if it is at either end of their row. The winner is the first child to turn over all five of their animals and call out *Loto !*

Key words

Core:

le rat – the rat
le bœuf – the ox
le tigre – the tiger
le lapin – the rabbit
le dragon – the dragon
le serpent – the snake
le cheval – the horse
la chèvre – the goat
le singe – the monkey
le coq – the cockerel
le chien – the dog
le cochon – the pig
les ciseaux (m) – scissors
la colle – the glue
les feutres (m) – felt-tip pens
distribue – give out (talking to one child)
distribuez – give out (talking to several children)
prenez – take
dessinez – draw
coupez – cut
pliez – fold
verticalement – vertically
horizontalement – horizontally

attachez – attach
collez – glue or stick (the action)
décorez – decorate
ouvrez – open
le papier (*rouge*) – (red) paper

Extension:

janvier – January
février – February
mars – March
avril – April
mai – May
juin – June
juillet – July
août – August
septembre – September
octobre – October
novembre – November
décembre – December
la ferme – the farm
la jungle – the jungle
la cave – cellar (false friend)
la caverne – cave
la grotte – grotto, cave
loto ! – Bingo!
choisis (sing) – choose
choisissez (pl) – choose

Key phrases

Core:

le nouvel an – New Year
Bonne année ! – Happy New Year!
Bonne année chinoise ! – Happy Chinese New Year!
l'horoscope (m) *chinois* – the Chinese horoscope
Vous allez faire ... – You are going to make...
une lanterne chinoise – a Chinese lantern

Extension:

Je suis né/née en (*2000*) – I was born in (2000)
Bonne chance ! – Good luck!
Le dragon, c'est un animal imaginaire – the dragon is an imaginary animal
le zodiac chinois – the Chinese horoscope
Je suis ... – I am...
L'animal habite ... – The animal lives...
dans la jungle – in the jungle
dans une ferme – on a farm

Language points

- In the word *bœuf* the letters 'o' and 'e' are joined; this blends the vowels. The children may have met the same spelling in the words *sœur* or *œuf*.
- (*Un*) *Chinois* (capital '*C*') is a Chinese person or the language; *chinois* (small '*c*') is the adjective.
- The suffix *-ment* on the end of a word signifies an adverb and corresponds to the English suffix '-ly', for example *horizontalement* and horizontally.
- Draw the children's attention to the verb *habiter*. Can they think of linked words in English?

Unit 6: Carnaval !

Objectives

To learn words and phrases related to *Carnaval* and *Mardi Gras*; to follow and understand a recipe in French.

Introducing the vocabulary

- Explain to the children that in France and other francophone countries, *Mardi Gras* and *Carnaval* have become almost synonymous.
- Ask the children if they have ever heard of *Mardi Gras*. Explain that traditionally, in the Christian calendar, *Mardi Gras* (meaning 'Fat Tuesday'), or Shrove Tuesday, is the day before Lent begins. During Lent it was once forbidden to eat meat or animal products, including eggs, hence '*Carne vale*' from the Latin meaning 'farewell to meat'. *Mardi Gras* was the day to eat up all fat and eggs before Lent which is why it is traditional to eat *crêpes*, just as we eat pancakes in the UK.

Core activities

- Today Carnaval is hugely popular throughout France and in other Catholic countries. There are parades, masked balls, special events and fireworks in many towns and cities throughout February and March. Children take part by wearing fancy dress.
- Show the children the 'Image: *Carnaval de Bailleul*' to give them a flavour of the festivities.
- Talk about pancakes. Have they ever made them? What do they think are the main ingredients? Explain how *crêpes* are very popular to eat in France throughout the year and that there are *crêperies* where you can buy *crêpes* containing all sorts of fillings, both sweet and savoury. Watch the 'Film: *La crêperie*'. How do the *crêpes* in the film vary from the pancakes they often have on Shrove Tuesday in the UK?
- Explain to the children that you are going to show them how to make a pancake batter (*la pâte à crêpes*). The English word 'batter' comes from the French word *battre* 'to beat'. How do they think the ingredients are mixed together?
- Go through the utensils one by one using 'Interactive flashcard: *Les ustensiles*'. Then go through the ingredients. Can the children find any similarities between the French and English words (*ingrédients*, *ustensiles*, *sel*, *sucre* etc)? What do they think *un saladier* is normally used for?
- Use 'Interactive activity: *Les ingrédients*' to reinforce the vocabulary. Double click on the French to hear it spoken.
- Make *crêpes* in the classroom if at all possible. Invite the children to taste some *crêpes*. Give the children the choice of lemon (*citron*) or jam (*confiture*).

Extension activities

- Explain to the children that they are going to be 'language detectives' by studying a French recipe.
- Distribute 'Photocopiable: *La pâte à crêpes*' from the CD-ROM. Ask the children to try to follow the text and also look at the pictures for clues about the recipe. Remind them that they already know quite a lot about *crêpe*-making which should help them.
- Distribute photocopiable page 37: (*Sois un détective de langue !*). Ask the children to look at the text and pictures again before reading the questions.
- Remind the children that this is a nine-step recipe and each of the boxes is about doing the next step.
- Go through the questions with the whole class or give the children time to complete the questions individually.
- When complete, go through their answers talking about the children's choices and possible alternatives.

Resources

Interactive flashcard:
Les ustensiles

Interactive activity:
Les ingrédients

Photocopiable:
La pâte à crêpes

Photocopiable page 37:
Sois un détective de langue !

Image:
Carnaval de Bailleul

Film: *La crêperie*

Preparation

Optional – ingredients and utensils for making *crêpes*, labelled in French: 110g plain flour, sifted; pinch of salt; two eggs; 200ml milk mixed with 75ml water; 50g butter (makes 12–14 *crêpes*)

Optional – an electric *crêpe* griddle or frying pan and cooker

Interactive whiteboard

Unit 6: Carnaval !

Cross-curricular ideas

Geography: To compare carnivals in different parts of the world.
If possible show photographs from carnival in different towns in francophone countries such as *Le Carnaval de Québec* in Canada; *Le Carnaval de Nice* in France; *Le Carnaval de Stavelot* in Belgium. Can they make any comparisons? Some children may have heard of the *Mardi Gras* carnival in New Orleans. If possible locate New Orleans on a map; explain to the children that *Orléans* is a big French town (show on the map of France) and New Orleans – or *La Nouvelle-Orléans* – was founded by the French.

Art and design: To design a mask for a masquerade ball.
It is often part of the traditions of carnival to masquerade or hold masquerade balls. Tell the children to find out about these traditions, in particular the different masks that are worn when masquerading. Children can then design their own masks.

Five-minute follow-ups

- Send for carnival posters from French and Belgian tourist offices. Contact tourist offices throughout France at **http://office-de-tourisme.net** or search for the name of a town plus *office de tourisme*. Show the children the packaging, stamps and handwriting before using the posters for display.

Key words

Core:

le carnaval – the carnival
le Mardi Gras – Mardi Gras ('Fat Tuesday')
une crêpe – a pancake
la farine – the flour
le sucre – the sugar
un œuf, deux œufs – an egg, two eggs
le lait – the milk
le sel – the salt
le beurre – the butter
un fouet – a whisk
une poêle – a frying pan
un verre gradué – a measuring jug
une balance – scales
un saladier – a big bowl, salad bowl
les ingrédients (m) – the ingredients
les ustensiles (m) – the utensils
le citron – the lemon
une petite cuillère – a teaspoon
la confiture – the jam

Extension:

une casserole – a pan

Key phrases

Core:

la pâte à crêpes – batter
je prépare la pâte – I prepare the batter
je mets – I put
je bats la pâte – I beat the batter
dans le saladier/dans le (grand) bol – in the (big) bowl
le beurre fondu – melted butter
je fais la crêpe – I make the pancake

Extension:

faire fondre – (to) melt
verser – (to) pour

ajouter – (to) add
(bien) mélanger – (to) mix (well)
faire un puits – (to) make a well
casser les œufs – (to) break the eggs
le beurre fondu – the melted butter
petit à petit – little by little
laisser reposer – (to) leave to rest
faire les crêpes – (to) make the pancakes
Bon appétit ! – eat well/enjoy your meal

Language points

- The instructions for the recipe are given as infinitives, eg *ajouter, casser, verser,* etc. This is common practice for recipes in French and avoids using the imperative. The use of the infinitive does not affect the meaning.
- There are many cognates or near cognates in both activities; try to draw out the similarities between the French and the English words.

Unit 7: Joyeuses Pâques !

Objectives

To know French words and phrases associated with Easter; to learn directional vocabulary and phrases; to follow instructions for a recipe.

Introducing the vocabulary

- Teach the children directions *gauche* and *droite* (left and right). Stand with your back to the children, to avoid confusion.
- Teach the verb *tourner* (to turn). Practise by giving directions to the whole class: *tournez à droite*; *tournez à gauche*. Ask one child to come to the front and give directions. Children could also practise this in pairs, but would need to use the singular imperative form *tourne*.
- Add the phrase: *Allez tout droit* (go straight on). Again, practise with different children as the leader and then in pairs. (The singular is *va*.)
- Use 'Interactive activity: *La chasse à l'œuf*' to reinforce directional language by helping the boy to find his Easter egg.

Vocabulary extension

- Add the phrase: *Prenez un pas/prenez deux pas* (take one/two steps). Ask the children how they would make different phrases to tell someone to turn left/right and take one/two/three steps. Remember to change to the singular imperative (*prends*) if talking to one child only.

Core activities

- Explain to the children that Easter is a Christian festival in France as it is elsewhere. The traditions of spring, growth and rebirth associated with Easter are also shared in francophone countries and the same symbols are used as in the UK – chocolate eggs and the Easter bunny.
- Explain how in francophone countries children leave a nest with a carrot in it, for the bunny, the night before Easter Sunday. During the night, the bunny finds it and then leaves eggs, which he has painted in different colours. When children wake in the morning they hunt for the coloured eggs.
- In Belgium, Switzerland and France, expert *chocolatiers* (chocolate chefs) make wonderful Easter eggs and other models.
- Use 'Interactive flashcard: *La chasse à l'œuf*' to practise some of the vocabulary connected with Easter traditions and symbols.
- Explain to the children that the *le lapin* or *le lièvre de Pâques* (Easter bunny) has hidden an egg in the classroom and that one child must find it.
- Choose one child to leave (*sors*) the room. Choose a second child to be *le lapin de Pâques*. He/she has to hide the egg, but make sure everyone knows where it is. Ask another child to fetch the one outside by saying: *Entre, s'il te plaît*.
- Children then take turns to give this child directions until he/she finds the egg – *Voilà !*

Extension activity

- Make *mendiants* following the recipe on photocopiable page 38 (*Mendiants au chocolat*). This is the cheapest, easiest type of traditional chocolate sweet to make. This activity will give rise to lots of talk in English or French about melting, setting, and solidifying. **Safety note: Care must be taken when using hot water in the classroom.**

Resources

Interactive flashcard:
La chasse à l'œuf

Interactive activity:
La chasse à l'œuf

Photocopiable page 38:
Mendiants au chocolat

Preparation

A real Easter egg or something to represent one

Ingredients and equipment for mendiants au chocolat: 300g dark chocolate; dried fruit; 50g butter; greaseproof paper; a large plate or flat tray; kettle; heatproof pan or bowl with a heatproof plate that sits on top; knife; spoon; access to a fridge

Interactive whiteboard

Tips

You can see lots of pictures of traditional Easter sweets if you put *mendiants au chocolat* into a search engine.

Cross-curricular ideas

Geography: To find out about chocolate production.

Ask children to find out more about chocolate and the links to francophone countries. Where are cocoa beans grown? Which countries are famous for chocolate-making?

Maths: To give and follow directions around a map or plan.

Write directions in French for getting from the school entrance to your classroom or another mystery area and follow them.

Five-minute follow-ups

Learn the rhyme *C'était Pâques*

C'était Pâques le matin	It was Easter in the morning
J'ai trouvé dans mon jardin	In my garden I found
Des œufs verts comme les prés	Green eggs like fields
Des œufs jaunes comme le soleil	Yellow eggs like the sun
Des œufs rouges comme les tulipes	Red eggs like tulips

- Ask the children to illustrate a display of the nouns from the Easter poem, with a green egg and a field, a yellow egg and the sun, and a red egg like tulips. They could then substitute other colours and objects, and add to the poem and the display following the same structure.
- Make a sign '*Joyeuses Pâques*' using different fonts. Show the children how to find accents used in different languages in Word.

Key words

Core:

droite – right
gauche – left
droit – straight on
première – first
deuxième – second
troisième – third
la rue – the road, street
le sentier – the path
un lapin – a rabbit
un lièvre – a hare
un œuf – an egg
un œuf de Pâques – an Easter egg
un nid – a nest
une carotte – a carrot
le chocolat – a/the chocolate
tourne/tournez – turn
prends/prenez – take
un pas – a step
va/allez – go
cache/cachez – hide
sors/sortez – go out
entre/entrez – come in
voilà ! – there it is!

Extension:

un bonbon – a sweet
un mendiant – a type of sweet; literally 'a beggar'
le beurre – the butter
faire fondre – to make something melt
chaud – hot
froid – cold

Key phrases

Core:

la chasse à l'œuf – Easter egg hunt
cachez l'œuf – hide the egg
l'œuf est caché – the egg is hidden
tournez à gauche – turn left
tournez à droite – turn right
allez tout droit – go straight on
prenez la première (rue) à droite – take the first (road) on the right
prenez la deuxième (rue) à droite – take the second (road) on the right
prenez la troisième (rue) à gauche – take the third (road) on the left
prenez un pas/deux pas/trois pas à gauche/droite – take one step/two steps/three steps to the left/right

Extension:

faites fondre – melt (imperative)
chauffez – heat
mettez – put
une assiette – a plate
un couteau – a knife
une cuillère – a spoon
un bol – a bowl
le papier sulfurisé – the greaseproof paper
en morceaux – in pieces
une assiette allant au flour – a heatproof plate

Language points

- It's very important to stress the pronunciation of the 't' sound in *droite* (right) but not in *droit* (straight on) or directions get very confused!
- To give directional instructions to one child only, change the verbs as follows: *tournez/tourne*; *cachez/cache*; *allez/va*; *prenez/prends*.

Unit 8: Des fêtes du printemps

Objectives

To find out about some French spring festivals and compare with festivals in the UK; to learn the prepositions *sur, sous, dans, devant, derrière*; **to learn weather conditions and seasons.**

Introducing the vocabulary

- Explain that in France it is the custom for children to stick paper fish on each other's backs and that *Poisson d'avril* is the phrase that French children call out when they have tricked someone.
- Use 'Interactive flashcard: *Poisson d'avril*' to reinforce the prepositions and introduce the core vocabulary relating to *Poisson d'avril*.

Vocabulary extension

- Explain that many words for weather are similar in French and English (cognates), for example *la température, le thermomètre* but are pronounced differently.

Core activities

- Try to do these activities on or as near as possible to 1 April. Write the date on the board in French. Ask the children to repeat '*C'est le premier avril*'.
- In English, ask the children what they do in the UK on April Fool's Day. Explain that in France the custom is slightly different. Write the phrase *Poisson d'avril* on the board. Can the children remember what this means?
- Distribute sheets of A5 card and ask the children to draw and cut out a fish outline. They should copy the words *Poisson d'avril* onto one side and write their names on the other side. Give each child a Velcro® dot or a piece of double-sided tape and ask them to place it near the top of the fish's head on the *Poisson d'avril* side.
- During the rest of the day the children can try to stick the fish on each others' backs. Explain that the trick lies in catching out unsuspecting victims. They will need to bide their time and not forget to say '*Poisson d'avril !*'

Extension activities

- Explain that in many French-speaking countries it is the custom on 1 May to offer a small bunch of lily of the valley (*le muguet*) to loved ones, to bring happiness for the coming year.
- Show the children the 'Image: *Muguet du bois*' from the CD-ROM. Explain that the white flowers are sweet-smelling.
- In France, lily of the valley is grown in great quantities for 1 May. If you have any growing in your garden bring some in to school to show the children. **Safety note: these plants are poisonous and children should not be allowed to touch them.**
- Lily of the valley may not always be found growing in the UK by 1 May as conditions in spring are not always ideal. Explain that weather conditions in France may differ from the UK especially in the south of France. *Why is this?*
- Use 'Interactive activity: *Quel temps fait-il aujourd'hui ?*' to reinforce different weather conditions. Introduce the four seasons and ask the children what the weather is like in each, for example: *Quel temps fait-il au printemps ? Il fait beau*.
- Using photocopiable page 39 (*Quel temps fait-il aujourdhui ?*) invite the children (individually or in groups) to fill in the relevant data. Collate the information and present in graphic form.

Cross-curricular ideas

Maths: To record weather data using graphs and charts.

Ask the children to use the completed weather charts to record weather over a period of time.

Resources

Interactive flashcard: *Poisson d'avril*

Interactive activity: *Quel temps fait-il aujourd'hui ?*

Photocopiable page 39: *Quel temps fait-il aujourd'hui ?*

Image: *Muguet du bois*

Preparation

Lily of the valley (optional) – see Safety note below

Items to make a card fish: card; coloured felt tip-pens; paper; scissors; double-sided tape or Velcro®

Large plastic bottles

Interactive whiteboard

Tips

Teach *sur, sous, dans, devant, derrière* by introducing this simple song to the tune of 'London Bridge is Falling Down':

Sur, sous, dans, devant, derrière devant, derrière devant derrière sur, sous, dans, devant, derrière où est le poisson ?

Accompany the song with gestures to show the meaning of the words.

Art and design: To make a greetings card.

Invite the children to make a greetings card for *la fête du muguet*, making detailed observational drawings of lilies of the valley.

D&T/Science: To make a rain gauge.

Challenge the children to use a large plastic bottle to design and make a rain gauge.

Five-minute follow-ups

- Use the children's fish to make a display or mobile. They can be embellished with scales (*des écailles*).
- Play a game of '*Où est le poisson ?*'. One child goes out of the room, another child hides the fish. The first child returns and tries to find the fish. *Chaud* and *froid* can be used for hot and cold.

Language points

- To say 'in a season' we say *en été, en automne, en hiver. Le printemps* is the odd one out: *au printemps*.
- The French say *dans le dos* or *sur le dos* for 'on the back'.
- Velcro® is a word derived from a combination of two French words: *velours* (velvet) and *crochet* (hook). Ask the children if they know why this word was chosen.
- Clues for the meaning of words beginning with 'e' acute (*é*) can often be given by substituting the letter *s*. Does this help the children to decipher the meaning of the word *écaille*?

Key words

Core:

le printemps – the spring
l'été (m) – the summer
l'automne (m) – the autumn
l'hiver (m) – the winter
la saison – the season
sur – on
sous – under
dans – in
devant – in front of
derrière – behind
le poisson – the fish
le velcro – the Velcro®

le scotch (*à double face*) – (double-sided) sellotape
chaud – hot
froid – cold
des écailles (f) – (fish) scales

Extension:

le muguet – lily of the valley
le thermomètre – thermometer
l'anémomètre (m) – anemometer, wind gauge

le degré (*celsius*) – degree (celsius)
la température – the temperature
le millilitre – millilitre
la pluie – the rain
le vent – the wind
le ciel – the sky
le nord – the north
le sud – the south
l'est (m) – the east
l'ouest (m) – the west
la neige – the snow
le soleil – the sun

Key phrases

Core:

Quelle est la date aujourd'hui ? – What is the date today?
(C'est) le premier avril – (It is) the first of April
Où est le poisson ? – Where is the fish?
Poisson d'avril ! – 'April fish' – no direct translation; said when children are 'got' by the fish on their back
dans le dos – on the back

Extension:

le premier mai – 1 May
la fête du muguet – The festival of lily of the valley

Quel temps fait-il aujourd'hui ? – What is the weather like today?
Il fait chaud – It is hot
Il fait froid – It is cold
Il fait beau – It is fine
Il fait mauvais – It is bad weather
Il fait du brouillard – It is foggy
Il y a du soleil – It is sunny
Il pleut – It is raining
Il y a des nuages – It is cloudy
Il gèle – It is freezing
Il fait (20) degrés – It is (20) degrees
Il fait moins (2) degrés – It is minus (2) degrees

Unit 9: La Fête Nationale

Objectives

To know French words and phrases associated with *La Fête Nationale* **(14th July); to learn words and phrases associated with drawing.**

Introducing the vocabulary

- Explain to the children that 14 July is the French national day and a national holiday. Introduce the name *La Fête Nationale* and tell the children it commemorates the day when the *Bastille* was stormed and the beginning of the French Revolution in 1789.
- If available, show the children the French *Tricolore* flag (*le drapeau Tricolore*).
- Explain to the children that there are usually military parades (*des défilés*), open-air dances (*des bals*) and fireworks (*des feux d'artifice*) to celebrate the day.
- Use 'Interactive flashcard: *La Fête Nationale*' showing a military parade to introduce some of the core vocabulary.
- Explain that through the Revolution, France ceased to be a monarchy and became a republic. Three words help to remember this: *le roi, la révolution, La République*. Allow the children to practise saying these words to bring out the 'r' sounds.

Vocabulary extension

- Practise saying the key phrases: *Vive la France !* and *Bonne fête !*

Core activities

- Encourage the children to find out as much as possible about the events that happen to celebrate *La Fête Nationale* using books and the internet.
- If possible, show the children film clips and/or photographs of *La Fête Nationale* celebrations (see **www.choletblog.fr**).
- Ask the children to make a small book about what they have found out about *La Fête Nationale*.
- Explain and practise the key words: *un défilé* (a parade), *un bal* (a dance), *un feu d'artifice* (a firework display) and suggest that these should be included in the illustrations.
- The books could also include information about French symbols or emblems. For example: *le Tricolore, la Marseillaise, la guillotine, Marie Antoinette, Marianne* (appears on stamps and coins).

Extension activities

- Before doing this activity take a good look at Claude Monet's painting of *La Rue Montorgueil* on the CD-ROM; do not share it with the children at this stage.
- Use 'Interactive activity: *Dictée illustrée*' to introduce the vocabulary used for drawing.
- Distribute paper and pencils and tell the children that you are going to ask them to create an impression – not an accurate drawing – of celebrations in Paris. (Give some information about Impressionism if appropriate.)
- Read out the instructions on photocopiable page 40 (*Dictée illustrée*) in French, using hand gestures to help (practise beforehand if possible).
- Finally reveal Monet's *La Rue Montorgueil* on the board and ask the children to compare their own and their neighbours' versions with the original.
- Later distribute the red and blue crayons/pastels and ask the children to add detail, still in the Impressionist style. Display the children's work alongside the *dictée illustrée* script.
- The photocopiable page can also be used for reading and understanding activities.

Resources

Interactive flashcard:
La Fête Nationale

Interactive activity:
Dictée illustrée

Photocopiable page 40:
Dictée illustrée

Image:
La Rue Montorgueil

Preparation

A4 paper for drawing and making small books; pencils; red and blue crayons/pastels

A *Tricolore* flag (optional)

Interactive whiteboard

Unit 9: La Fête Nationale

Cross-curricular ideas

Music: To listen to and accompany the *Marseillaise*.

Listen to a recording of the *Marseillaise*. The words will be too difficult for the children but they could try humming along or beating along with the rhythm using classroom percussion instruments.

Five-minute follow-ups

- Explain the French national motto: *Liberté, Égalité, Fraternité*. Allow the children to practise saying it to bring out the sound of the final 'e' acute (*é*).
- Mount a classroom display of symbols of France.
- Explain that the metric system began in the time of the French Revolution; give practice in saying and using different measures.

Key words

Core:
un défilé – a parade
un bal – a dance
un feu d'artifice – a firework; a firework display
la Marseillaise – the *Marseillaise* (French national anthem)
le roi – the king
la révolution – the revolution
La République (française)– the (French) Republic

à gauche – on the left
à droite – on the right
le triangle – the triangle
une fenêtre – a window
un balcon – a balcony
là – there
aussi – also
des hommes (m) – men
des femmes (f) – women
des enfants (m) – children
des familles (f) – families

Extension:
une ligne (*verticale/ diagonale*) – a (vertical/diagonal) line
tracez – draw (a line)
un coin – a corner
une croix – a cross
dessinez – draw
un nuage – a cloud

Key phrases

Core:
vous avez – you (pl) have
au milieu de – in the middle of
c'est une grande rue à Paris – it is a big street in Paris
il fait beau – it is fine (weather)
il fait du vent – it is windy
il y a beaucoup de drapeaux Tricolores – there are a lot of Tricolore flags
qui dansent dans le vent – which dance in the wind
ils sont très, très petits – they are very, very small
La Fête Nationale – the National Day
il y a beaucoup de gens – there are a lot of people

Extension:
Vive la France ! – Long live France!
Bonne fête ! – Enjoy the festival! (no direct translation)
Liberté, Égalité, Fraternité – Liberty, Equality, Fraternity (French national motto)

Language points

- Many of the words in the main activity are cognates: they are the same or similar to English words. Draw the children's attention to this as an aid to understanding.
- Imperatives (commands) of *-er* verbs end in *-ez* when addressing the whole class, for example *tracez, dessinez*.
- *Beaucoup de* is an expression of quantity meaning 'a lot of' or 'many'.

Unit 10: Aïd Mubarak !

Objectives

To know French words and phrases associated with the Muslim community in the francophone world; to use colour adjectives; to learn some imperative verbs.

Introducing the vocabulary

- Use the text on photocopiable page 41 (*Connaissances de base*) to talk about the religious festival of Eid. Highlight some of the core vocabulary, for example: *Aïd al-Fitr, la mosquée, ramadan.*
- Explain that the children will be making an Eid card by following instructions in French. Introduce some of the verbs that they will need to know. Say the words and show the children actions for each of the following verbs:

  regardez – look
  pliez – fold
  posez – put
  dessinez – draw
  copiez – copy
  collez – stick

- Use 'Interactive activity: *Les impératifs*' to reinforce the vocabulary.
- Ask the children to practise the words and actions in pairs.
- Look at 'Interactive flashcard: *Une mosquée*'. Point out the architectural features and find out the French names by clicking on the hot spots. Use the phrase *C'est ...* (*une mosquée/un minaret*). Encourage the children to notice the similarities between the English and French names.

Vocabulary extension

- To differentiate, you could add colours and positions, for example: *Il y a un dôme doré en haut/il y a un minaret noir en haut/il y a une porte verte en bas*.

Core activities

- Point out that many francophone countries are Islamic. Explain to the children that the most important festival for the Muslim year is called *Aïd al-Fitr*, which we call Eid el Fitr. Find out what real mosques in francophone countries look like by visiting **www.travel-images.com/mosques.html**
- Tell the children they are going to make an Eid card. Explain that the instructions will be in French, but you will hold up all the objects you are talking about and you will repeat the instructions several times. They should listen carefully for words they know already, or that sound like English.
- Continue to do the actions as you read the text from photocopiable page 42 (*Une carte d'Aïd*). (A translation of the instructions is available on the CD-ROM.)

Extension activities

- Make a larger mosque silhouette for a display. Label the different parts as: *le dôme, le minaret, la porte, la fenêtre*.
- Practise using positional language such as *en haut; dans la partie inférieure*.

Cross-curricular ideas

Geography: To find out about some of the francophone countries in the world.
Locate some of the French-speaking countries listed in the Extension key words on a globe or atlas.
Find out which ones have Muslim populations. Investigate them at **www.maps4free.com**

Resources

Interactive flashcard:
Une mosquée

Interactive activity:
Les impératifs

Photocopiable page 41:
Connaissances de base

Photocopiable page 42:
Une carte d'Aïd

Translation:
Une carte d'Aïd

Preparation

Globe/world map

Materials to make a card: blue A4 card and black A5 card; green felt or soft paper; small pieces of silver/gold paper; glue; scissors

Interactive whiteboard

Tips

Visit the Paris mosque at **www.mosquee-de-paris.org** Find out the dates of religious festivals including Eid by selecting '*Fêtes religieuses*' from the '*Infos pratiques*' menu.

Five-minute follow-ups

- Ask the children to work in pairs to practise this dialogue for introducing themselves to a child from another country:

  D'où viens-tu ? – Where are you from?

  Je viens de ... – I come from...

  Quelle langue parles-tu ? – What language do you speak?

  Je parle ... – I speak....

  Quelle est ta nationalité ? – What nationality are you?

  Je suis (anglais/e) – I am... (English)

- Find the flags of each Islamic francophone country at **www.cyber-flag.net** Ask the children if they know any French people whose families came from these countries (clue: think of footballers).

Key words

Core:

regardez – look

pliez – fold

dessinez – draw

posez – put

copiez – copy

collez – stick

coupez – cut

une mosquée – a mosque

un dôme – a dome

un bulbe – an onion dome

un minaret – a minaret

une silhouette – a silhouette

la lune – the moon

vert – green

bleu – blue

argent – silver

doré – golden

Extension:

trouvez – find

le monde – the world

un pays – a country

voici (le Maroc) – here is (Morocco)

le Maroc – Morocco

la Tunisie – Tunisia

l'Algérie (f) – Algeria

le Mali – Mali

le Sénégal – Senegal

la Côte d'Ivoire – Ivory Coast

le Cameroun – Cameroon

la nationalité – the nationality

la langue – the language

Key phrases

Core:

C'est un/une ... It's a

Il y a ... – There is, there are ...

en haut – high up

en bas – at the bottom

la partie inférieure – the lower part

Aïd Mubarak ! – Eid Mubarak! (happy Eid!)

Extension:

Où sont les pays islamiques francophones ? – Where are the French-speaking Muslim countries?

D'où viens-tu ? – Where do you come from?

Quelle langue parles-tu ? – What language do you speak?

Quelle est ta nationalité ? – What is your nationality?

Je viens de ... – I come from...

Je parle ... – I speak...

Je suis anglaise ... – I am English

Language points

- Note the words that are the same or similar in both English and French (cognates) – *mosque/une mosquée* ; *dome/un dôme* ; *minaret/un minaret* ; *silhouette/une silhouette*.

- Imperatives used in instructions can be recognised by their *–ez* endings, eg *collez* ; *coupez*.

- Colour adjectives come after the noun and most colours have to agree, for example *la carte bleue, un crayon blanc*. However *rouge, rose, marron* and *orange* always stay the same.

- Country names have capital letters but nationality, language and months do not, for example: *En France, les français parlent français* ; *l'Aïd est en septembre*.

- Words with circumflexes (eg *dôme*) the circumflex usually means there used to be an 's' in the spelling but makes no difference to pronunciation.

Unit 11: Joyeux anniversaire !

Objectives

To learn the months of the year; to learn numbers to 31.

Introducing the vocabulary

- Over time introduce numbers 1 to 31 and the months of the year. Gradually build this into the daily routine of the class so that they are used to the question *Quelle est la date aujourd'hui ?* and can respond.
- Use 'Interactive flashcard: *Les mois de l'année*' to reinforce the children's knowledge of the months of the year.

Vocabulary extension

- Introduce *je suis né(e) en* ... and challenge the children to say when they were born.
- Explain that we use the word *née* in English when it means 'born'. Show them an example of the births section of a newspaper and ask them if they can work out what it means when used in this way (mother's maiden name).

Core activities

- Teach the children how to answer the question *Quel âge as-tu ?*' (How old are you?) and allow them to practise answering saying '*J'ai ... ans*'.
- Explain to the children that they are going to learn how to say when their birthday is by listening to a song. Play the 'Song: *Quelle est la date de ton anniversaire ?*' from the CD-ROM once or twice. Ask the children to suggest what the question is. (A translation of the song is available on the CD-ROM).
- Challenge the children to answer the question with their knowledge about numbers and months. They could answer: *C'est le ... Mon anniversaire est ...*
- Use 'Interactive activity: *Quelle est la date de ton anniversaire ?*' to drag and drop the dates to the correct birthdays. Double click on the text to hear it spoken.

Extension activities

- Distribute photocopiable page 43 (*Les mois et les nombres*) and ask the children to cut out the date and number captions. In pairs, ask the children to make up a date with the captions and each child asks the other *Quelle est la date de ton anniversaire ?* Remind the children that they will need to use *premier* for 'first'.
- Tell the children that you are going to teach them how to say the year of their birth. Explain that although this is a big number they are really lucky because they have been born since 2000! Introduce *deux mille* and explain that all they need to do is add the final digit(s), for example *deux mille trois*. The phrase they need is *Je suis né(e) en* ... (*né* for boys; *née* for girls).

Cross-curricular ideas

Maths: To collect and record data.

Ask the children to find out the birthdays of the whole class. Record this information in a bar chart graph and label it in French. *Which month has the most birthdays? Are there any months where there are no birthdays?*

Literacy: To use a dictionary and develop knowledge about language.

Explain to the children that *premier* is often used in English too. Can they give any examples: premier league, premiership, film premiere? Explain links with 'prime', for example prime minister, prime numbers. Use dictionaries to look up more words if appropriate. (In both French and English the word comes from the Latin.)

Music: To practise singing in unison.

Use photocopiable page 44 (*Quelle est la date de ton anniversaire ?*) to learn to sing a birthday song.

Resources

Interactive flashcard: *Les mois de l'année*

Interactive activity: *Quelle est la date de ton anniversaire ?*

Photocopiable page 43: *Les mois et les nombres*

Photocopiable page 44: *Quelle est la date de ton anniversaire ?*

Song: *Quelle est la date de ton anniversaire ?*

Translation: *Quelle est la date de ton anniversaire ?*

Preparation

Date chart; calendar or poster

Interactive whiteboard

Five-minute follow-ups

- Explain that numbers do not always look the same when they are written in French, for example the one has a long tail on it and the seven is crossed through. Show the children examples if possible and invite them to practise for themselves.
- Tell the children your birth date, or that of a celebrity, in French and see if they can work out what it might be. Write their answers on mini whiteboards.
- Teach the children how to sing 'Happy Birthday' in French:

  Joyeux anniversaire
  Joyeux anniversaire
  Joyeux anniversaire
  Joyeux anniversaire

  You could simplify this to *Bon anniversaire* if you prefer.
- Make a class birthday chart for display.

Key words

Core:

dix – 10	*vingt* – 20	*trente* – 30	*juin* – June
un – 1	*onze* – 11	*vingt et un* – 21	*trente et un* – 31	*juillet* – July
deux – 2	*douze* – 12	*vingt-deux* – 22	*le premier* – the first	*août* – August
trois – 3	*treize* – 13	*vingt-trois* – 23	*la première* (f) – the first	*septembre* – September
quatre – 4	*quatorze* – 14	*vingt-quatre* – 24		*octobre* – October
cinq – 5	*quinze* – 15	*vingt-cinq* – 25	*janvier* – January	*novembre* – November
six – 6	*seize* – 16	*vingt-six* – 26	*février* – February	*décembre* – December
sept – 7	*dix-sept* – 17	*vingt-sept* – 27	*mars* – March	
huit – 8	*dix-huit* – 18	*vingt-huit* – 28	*avril* – April	
neuf – 9	*dix-neuf* – 19	*vingt-neuf* – 29	*mai* – May	

Key phrases

Core:

Les mois de l'année – the months of the year

Quelle est la date aujourd'hui ? – What is the date today?

(Aujourd'hui) c'est le (cinq avril) – (Today) it's the (5th of April)

Quel âge as-tu ? – How old are you?

J'ai ... ans – I am...years old

Quelle est la date de ton anniversaire ? – When is your birthday? (What date is your birthday?)

Mon anniversaire est le ... – My birthday is on the...

Joyeux/Bon anniversaire ! – Happy birthday!

Extension:

En quelle année es-tu né(e) ? – In what year were you born?

Je suis né(e) en ...(2000) – I was born in...(2000)

Language points

- Ordinal numbers are not used for dates other than the first of the month.
- In French the first letter of the month is normally written in lower case, for example *avril*. (It may sometimes be capitalised in posters etc.)
- There is no word for 'on' when giving the date. For example, *mon anniversaire est le cinq avril* can mean 'my birthday is on the 5 April'. Children sometimes have difficulty with this.
- Because *anniversaire* begins with a vowel *joyeux* is pronounced differently so that *joyeux* sounds like *joyeuse* even though it is masculine.

Unit 12: La fête de la Musique

Objectives

To learn words and phrases associated with music; to perform a song in French; to find out about cultural events in France and francophone countries.

Introducing the vocabulary

- Find out who plays which instruments in the class. Introduce the vocabulary for the different instruments and teach *je joue du/de la/des ...* (I play the...). Don't forget to include: *je chante* (I sing) and *nous chantons* (we sing) as well as *je danse* (I dance) and *nous dansons* (we dance).
- Point out the words which are the same or very similar in English (cognates).
- Use 'Interactive flashcard: *Le groupe rock*' to practise the vocabulary.
- Using school instruments, children's own instruments or pictures of different instruments, ask: *Qu'est ce-que c'est ?* Encourage the children to respond in complete sentences: *C'est un/une ...*
- Use 'Interactive activity: *Les instruments musicaux*' to drag and drop the appropriate name to each instrument. Double click on the French to hear it spoken.

Core activities

- Explain to the children that festivals do not have to be religious. There are often festivals to celebrate particular activities, or foodstuffs, or the arts. Tell the children about *la fête de la Musique* started by the French government in 1982. It is always held on or around 21 June, the summer solstice. All performances are free, whether by famous musicians or amateur groups.
- Tell the children that you are going to hold your own *fête de la Musique* during an assembly.
- Teach the 'Song: *Gugusse*' from the CD-ROM and photocopiable page 45. (A translation of the song is also available on the CD-ROM.) Once the children know the song, you can substitute different instruments in the verses and children who play that instrument can stand forward with their instrument. For the performance you will also need a child to introduce *la fête de la Musique* to the audience, explaining that it is a celebration of music.
- Children who play their own instrument can say *je joue ...* and play a few notes. You can also add school percussion instruments and a group of dancers who could introduce themselves by saying *nous dansons !*

Extension activities

- Ask the children to research other secular festivals in France. Many are based on local food specialities. Tell the children they can find out what food is being celebrated and where, by typing the following terms into a search engine and looking for images: *la fête du citron à Menton, la fête de la tomate à Marmande, la fête de l'ail, la fête de la carotte à Croissy sur Sein, la fête de la mirabelle à Metz.*
- Explain to the children that there are hundreds of different regional festivals. Ask them to locate where the festivals they find take place, and mark an outline map of France with a symbol, for example a lemon on the south coast at *Menton*.

Cross-curricular ideas

Art and design: To design a poster.

Make posters in French to advertise your assembly performance. Don't forget to include the day and the time in French as well.

Music: To listen to and identify different musical instruments.

Visit **www.calabashmusic.com** to listen to extracts of music from all over the francophone world. Using the instrument flashcards and French vocabulary they have learned, challenge the children to identify the instruments they hear.

Resources

Interactive flashcard: *Le groupe rock*

Interactive activity: *Les instruments musicaux*

Photocopiable page 45: *Gugusse*

Song: *Gugusse*

Translation: *Gugusse*

Preparation

Pictures of different musical instruments or actual instruments (children could bring in their own)

Interactive whiteboard

Five-minute follow-ups

- Play the game *Jaques a dit* (Simon says) asking the children to pretend to play different musical instruments, for example *Jacques a dit jouez du piano !/ Jouez de la flûte !*
- Learn the action rhyme *Avec ma bouche*

Je mange avec ma bouche	I eat with my mouth
Tout ce qui est bon	Everything that's good.
Mes oreilles font pareil	My ears do the same
Elles mangent les sons	They eat sounds
Écoutons, écoutons	Let's listen, let's listen
Ce que les bruits font	To what the sounds do

- Listen to different genres of music. Identify them in English, and in French as *la musique jazz/la musique classique/le rock/le rap* and so on.

Key words

Core:

la fête (de) – the festival or celebration (of)

la musique – music

le solstice – midsummer day

le vingt et un juin – 21 June

la flûte –the flute

le hautbois – the oboe

la clarinette – the clarinet

le basson – the bassoon

la flûte à bec – the recorder

le saxophone – the saxophone

le cor – the horn

la trompette – the trumpet

le trombone – the trombone

le violon – the violin

le violoncelle – the cello

la contrebasse – the double bass

la guitare (électrique) – the (electric) guitar

le clavier – the keyboard

le piano – the piano

les castagnettes (f) – the castanets

les cymbales (f) – the cymbals

le tambour – the drum

la batterie – the drum kit

le glockenspiel – the glockenspiel

le marimba – the marimba

Key words

les maracas (m) – the maracas

le tambourin – the tambourine

le xylophone – the xylophone

l'orchestre (m) – the orchestra

le chœur d'enfants – the children's choir

l'instrument (m) – the instrument

la voix – the voice

le chanteur/la chanteuse (m/f) – the singer

Extension:

fêter – to celebrate

visiter – to visit

entrer – to go in

un citron – a lemon

une tomate – a tomato

de l'ail (m) – garlic

une carotte – a carrot

une mirabelle – a plum

(dans le) nord – (in the) north

(dans l') est – (in the) east

(dans le) sud – (in the) south

(dans l') ouest – (in the) west

Key phrases

Core:

Bienvenue à notre concert ! – Welcome to our concert!

je joue du/de la/des ... – I play the...

je chante – I sing...

nous chantons – we sing...

je danse – I dance

nous dansons – we dance

entrée gratuite – entrance free

nous allons jouer ... – we are going to play...

nous allons chanter ... – we are going to sing...

Extension:

Qu'est-ce qu'on fête ? – What are they, we celebrating?

On fête l'ail ! – They're, we're celebrating garlic!

Où est la fête de la mirabelle ? – Where is the plum festival?

C'est à Metz, dans l'est – It's at Metz, in the east

Language points

- Children will notice that most French names for musical instruments are the same as or very similar to English ones (cognates). However, watch out for the false cognate *organe* which refers to the organs of the body. Organ, the musical instrument, is *orgue*. *Trombone* on the other hand is the same, but also means 'paper clip'. Can the children work out why?
- French schools do not usually have assemblies so you will have to call your performance a concert.
- If the instrument is a masculine noun, eg *le piano,* the phrase you need is *je joue du piano*. If it is a feminine noun, eg *la flûte* the phrase is *je joue de la flûte*. If it is a plural eg *les cymbales*, the phrase is *je joue des cymbales*.

Le conte de Rama et Sita

Cast

le (vieux) roi
la (vieille) reine
Rama
Sita
Hanouman, le dieu-singe
le vieillard/Ravana, le monstre à dix têtes
l'armée des singes et les démons
les narrateurs

Narrateur 1 : (Say or hold up a card.) *Première scène – le palais.*

(Enter the old king, old queen, Rama and Sita. The old king is very tired. He is falling asleep on his throne.)

Le roi/la reine/Rama/Sita : *Nous sommes dans le palais.*

Le roi : *Je suis le roi. Je suis fatigué.*

La reine : *Je suis la reine.* (Pointing at Rama and Sita.) *Je vous déteste. Partez !*

Narrateur 2 : (Say or hold up a card.) *Scène deux – la forêt.*

Rama/Sita : *Nous sommes dans la forêt.*

Rama : *Je vais à la chasse.* (Exit Rama.)

(Sita is doing some gardening. Enter the old man.)

Le vieillard : (Chuckling wickedly.) *Je suis le vieillard. J'ai soif.*

(Sita gives him a drink. The old man suddenly turns into a ten-headed monster.)

Le vieillard/Ravana : *Je me transforme en Ravana ! J'enlève Sita !*

Sita : *Au secours !* (Sita continues to shout Au secours ! throughout the next scene.)

Narrateur 3 : (Say or hold up a card.) *Scène trois – l'île.*

Sita/Ravana : (Sita is crying. Ravana is chuckling.) *Nous sommes dans l'île.*

(Enter Hanuman.)

Hanouman : *Je suis Hanouman. Je cherche Sita !*

(Enter Rama.)

Rama/Hanouman : *Nous voyons Sita !*

Rama : *Je tue Ravana !*

(Enter the monkey army and demons.)

L'armée des singes : *Nous sommes l'armée des singes. Nous nous battons avec les démons !*

(Demons and monkey army fight. Monkey army wins.)

Narrateur 4 : (Say or hold up a card.) *Scène quatre – la ville.*

Rama/Sita : *Nous retournons à la ville.*

Narrateur 5 : (Say or hold up a card.) *Bienvenue à la ville !*

Rama/Sita : *Nous sommes dans le palais.*

Rama : *Je suis le (nouveau) roi.*

Sita : *Je suis la (nouvelle) reine.*

Illustration © 2010, Jackie Stafford/Beehive Illustration

La Ménorah de Hanoucca

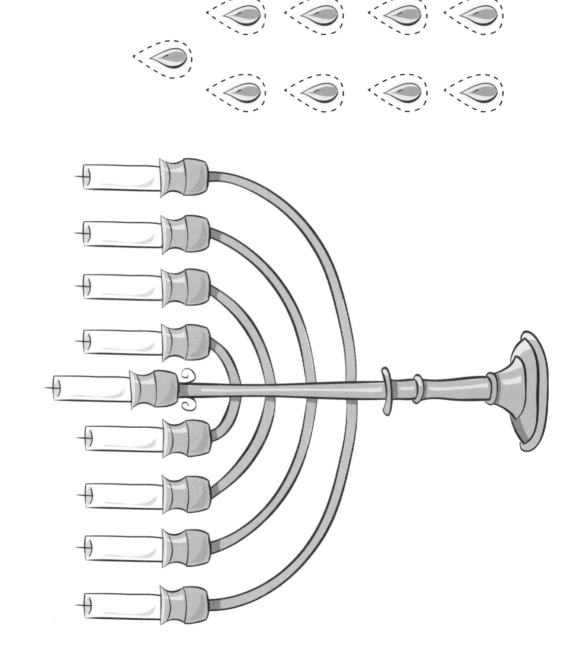

La fête des Rois

Aujourd'hui, la date c'est le six janvier. En France c'est la fête des Rois. Nous mangeons un gâteau spécial.

Les parents boivent du champagne et, parce que c'est une fête, les enfants boivent un tout petit peu aussi.

Le gâteau s'appelle la galette des Rois ; c'est délicieux !

Il y a une tranche de galette pour chaque personne.

> Dans certaines familles, le plus petit enfant va **sous la table**.

Dans la galette, il y a une fève. La personne qui trouve la fève est le roi ou la reine et porte une couronne aujourd'hui.

Questions

1. What is the date? _____

2. What is the special cake called? _____

3. It is a special occasion. What do people drink? _____

4. In the film, the boy found a small figure of a footballer. What word can you find that might be

   the French word for the small figure? _____

5. Can you find the French word for crown?

   _____

6. Look at the sentence inside the box. What do you think happens

   in some families (key words are highlighted to help you)?

   _____

   _____

Prénom :

Sois un détective de langue !

○ Look at the *crêpe* recipe and see if you can work out some of the instructions.

1. Can you guess what the word *fondre* means? (**Clue:** have you tried chocolate fondue?)

    Answer: _____

2. Can you think of an English word for *verser*? (**Clue:** what is being done to the flour?)

    Answer: _____

3. *Ajouter* means something different. What? (**Clue:** one ingredient is already in the bowl.)

    Answer: _____

4. What do you think *mélanger* means? (**Clue:** there is a spoon in the bowl.)

    Answer: _____

5. *Faire un puits* is really tricky! Any guesses?

    Answer: _____

6. *Casser* can be guessed by looking at the next two words in the sentence.

    Answer: _____

7. You have already met a similar word to *fondu* ; what do you think *beurre fondu* means?

    Answer: _____

8. *Petit à petit* shouldn't be too difficult! (**Clue:** *le lait* is milk.)

    Answer: _____

9. *Laisser reposer* is tricky! (**Clue:** does the time give a clue?)

    Answer: _____

10. There is no direct equivalent for *Bon appétit* in English. Can you make a suggestion?

    Answer: _____

Mendiants au chocolat

(Makes 30 small sweets)

Ingrédients

300g de chocolat noir – dark chocolate

Fruits secs coupés en morceaux – dried fruit, cut in pieces

50g de beurre – butter

papier sulfurisé – greaseproof paper

une assiette – a plate

une assiette allant au four – a heatproof plate

une bouilloire – kettle

un bol – a bowl

une cuillère – a spoon

un réfrigérateur– a fridge

○ Beurrez légèrement du papier sulfurisé.

○ Mettez le papier sur une assiette au réfrigérateur.

○ Cassez le chocolat noir en petits morceaux.

○ Mettez le chocolat sur une assiette allant au four.

○ Chauffez de l'eau dans une bouilloire.

○ Mettez l'eau chaude dans un bol.

○ Mettez l'assiette en dessus du bol pour faire fondre le chocolat.

○ Sortez l'assiette froide du réfrigérateur.

○ Immédiatement, formez des petits tas de chocolat sur le papier sulfurisé avec une cuillère.

○ Ajoutez des morceaux de fruit sec bien vite pendant que le chocolat reste fondu.

○ Lightly butter the greaseproof paper.

○ Put the paper on a plate in the fridge.

○ Break the dark chocolate into small pieces.

○ Put the chocolate onto a heatproof plate.

○ Boil the water in a kettle.

○ Put the hot water in a bowl.

○ Put the plate above the bowl to melt the chocolate.

○ Take the cold plate from the fridge.

○ Immediately make little mounds of chocolate on the greaseproof paper with a spoon.

○ Add pieces of dried fruit quickly, while the chocolate is still melted.

Prénom :

Quel temps fait-il aujourd'hui ?

La date : _____

Le jour : _____

La température à _____ heures : _____

La température à midi : _____

La température à _____ heures : _____

Le vent arrive

du nord   du sud   de l'est   de l'ouest

La pluie : _____ millilitres

Le ciel est

gris   bleu

Le temps aujourd'hui (sommaire) : _____

_____

_____

_____

_____

Dictée illustrée

○ Read these drawing clues in French to the children using hand gestures to help with meaning.
○ Remind them that they are to create an impression rather than an accurate drawing.

1. *Tracez deux lignes diagonales : une ligne d'un coin à l'autre coin. Vous avez une croix.*
2. *Au milieu de la page dessinez deux rectangles verticaux.*
3. *C'est une grande rue à Paris.*
4. *Il fait beau, le ciel est bleu et il y a deux nuages.*
5. *Dans le triangle à gauche, tracez beaucoup de lignes verticales et horizontales. Là, il y a des fenêtres et des balcons.*
6. *Il fait du vent aussi. Il y a beaucoup de drapeaux Tricolores qui dansent dans le vent.*
7. *Dans le triangle à droite il y a aussi beaucoup de drapeaux Tricolores : bleu, blanc et rouge.*
8. *Dans la rue il y a beaucoup de personnes : des hommes, des femmes, des enfants, des familles. Ils sont très, très petits !*

1. Draw two diagonal lines: from one corner to the other. You have drawn a cross.
2. In the middle of the page draw two vertical rectangles.
3. It is a large street in Paris.
4. It's fine, the sky is blue and there are two clouds.
5. In the left-hand triangle, draw lots of vertical and horizontal lines. These are windows and balconies.
6. It is also windy. There are many Tricolore flags dancing in the wind.
7. In the right-hand triangle there are also a lot of Tricolore flags: blue, white and red.
8. In the street there are lots of people: men, women, children, families. They are very, very small.

Connaissances de base

Il y a 5–6 millions de musulmans qui habitent en France. Il y a aussi beaucoup de pays musulmans où on parle français, parce que dans le passé les français les gouvernaient.

Les musulmans prient cinq fois par jour chez eux, au travail, ou dans les mosquées. Le moment le plus important de l'année pour eux est le mois de « ramadan ». Au cours de ramadan, ils ne mangent pas pendant la journée, et ils donnent de la charité aux pauvres. A la fin de ramadan il y a une fête très importante qui s'appelle l'Aïd al-Fitr, et deux mois plus tard la fête de l'Aïd al Adha. Les musulmans prient à la mosquée, se rendent visite en famille, donnent des cadeaux, et mangent un bon repas.

There are 5–6 million Muslims living in France. There are also several Islamic countries where French is spoken, because in the past these countries were governed by France.

Muslims pray five times a day, at home, at work, or at the mosque. The most important part of their year is the month of Ramadan. During Ramadan, they fast during daylight hours, and they give to charity. At the end of Ramadan there is a festival called Eid el Fitr, followed two months later by Eid el Adha. Muslims pray at the mosque, make family visits, give presents and eat a celebration meal.

Illustration © 2010, Jackie Stafford Beehive Illustration

Une carte d'Aïd

○ Read these instructions in French to the children using hand gestures to help with meaning.

○ Say: *Faites une carte d'Aïd pour envoyer à un ami/une amie.*

1. *Pliez la carte bleue en deux horizontalement pour faire un rectangle.* (Hold up blue card.)

2. *Collez du feutre vert en bas.* (Mime sticking on green felt.)

3. *Coupez la lune du papier argenté.* (Show silver crescent shape.)

4. *Collez-la en haut de la carte bleue.* (Mime with glue.)

5. *Coupez la silhouette de la mosquée.* (Show cutting out whole shape.)

6. *Posez la silhouette de la mosquée sur la carte noire.* (It's a good idea to demonstrate this, aligning the bottom and left-hand edges with the straight edges of the black card.)

7. *Dessinez autour de la silhouette avec un crayon blanc.*
   (Draw round it on black card with white pencil.)

8. *Coupez la silhouette. Avec une règle et le crayon blanc, redessinez les deux lignes horizontales pour marquer les deux sections horizontales.*
   (Draw in the horizontal white dotted lines.)

9. *Coupez la forme des fenêtres et d'une porte du papier doré ou argenté.*
   (Show another card with pieces stuck on.)

10. *Collez-les sur la silhouette de la mosquée.* (Mime with glue.)

11. *Pliez la silhouette aux deux lignes horizontales.* (Fold along horizontal lines.)

12. *Collez la section inférieure sur la partie verte de la carte.* (Glue lowest section and stick onto 'grass'.) *Voilà une mosquée en 3D ! Maintenant, écrivez à l'intérieur :*

○ Write the greeting message below on the board to help the children to complete their cards.

Cher/chère ...   (Depending on whether your friend is male or female.)

Aïd Mubarak !

Amitiés de,

Les mois et les nombres

un	deux	trois	quatre
cinq	six	sept	huit
neuf	dix	onze	douze
treize	quatorze	quinze	seize
dix-sept	dix-huit	dix-neuf	vingt
vingt et un	vingt-deux	vingt-trois	vingt-quatre
vingt-cinq	vingt-six	vingt-sept	vingt-huit
vingt-neuf	trente	trente et un	le premier
janvier	février	mars	avril
mai	juin	juillet	août
septembre	octobre	novembre	décembre

Quelle est la date de ton anniversaire ?

Quelle est la date de ton anniversaire ?
Quelle est la date de ton anniversaire ?

Janvier, février, mars ?
Janvier, février, mars ?

Quelle est la date de ton anniversaire ?
Quelle est la date de ton anniversaire ?

Avril, mai, juin ?
Avril, mai, juin ?

Janvier !
Février !
Mars !
Avril !
Mai !
Juin !
Juillet !
Août !
Septembre !
Octobre !
Novembre !
Décembre !

Quelle est la date de ton anniversaire ?
Quelle est la date de ton anniversaire ?

Juillet, août, septembre ?
Juillet, août, septembre ?

Quelle est la date de ton anniversaire ?
Quelle est la date de ton anniversaire ?

Octobre, novembre, décembre ?
Octobre, novembre, décembre ?

Ça y est !

Gugusse

C'est Gugusse avec son violon

Qui fait danser les filles

Qui fait danser les filles

C'est Gugusse avec son violon

Qui fait danser les filles

Et les garçons

Mon papa ne veut pas

Que je danse, que je danse

Mon papa ne veut pas

Que je danse la polka

Il dira ce qu'il voudra

Moi je danse, moi je danse

Il dira ce qu'il voudr

Moi je danse la polka

Glossary

General vocabulary

Everyday phrases and introductions

Je suis/nous sommes ...
.... I am/we are...
Quel âge as-tu ? .... How old are you?
J'ai ... ans .... I am...years old
Quelle est la date de ton anniversaire ?
.... When is your birthday?
Mon anniversaire est le ...
.... My birthday is on the...
En quelle année es-tu né(e) ?
.... In what year were you born?
Je suis né(e) en (2000)
.... I was born in...(2000)
D'où viens-tu ? ..... Where do you come from?
Je viens de ... . I come from...
Quelle langue parles-tu ?
.... What language do you speak?
Je parle ... . I speak...
Quelle est ta nationalité ?
.... What is your nationality?
Je suis anglais(e) ... I am English

Topic-related vocabulary

Animals

agneau (m) .... lamb
âne (m) .... donkey
bœuf (m) .... ox
chameau (m) ...... camel
cheval (m) .... horse
chèvre (f) .... goat
chien (m) .... dog
cochon (m) .... pig
coq (m) .... cockerel
dragon (m) .... dragon
lapin (m) .... rabbit
lièvre (m) .... hare
mouton (m) .... sheep
nid (m) .... nest
poisson (m) .... fish
rat (m) .... rat
serpent (m) .... snake
singe (m) .... monkey
tigre (m) .... tiger
L'animal habite dans la jungle/dans une ferme
.... The animal lives in the jungle/on the farm

Calendar

janvier .... January
février .... February
mars .... March
avril .... April
mai .... May
juin .... June
juillet .... July
août .... August
septembre .... September
octobre .... October
novembre .... November
décembre .... December
printemps (m)...... spring
été (m) .... summer
automne (m)....... autumn
hiver (m).......... winter
saison (f) .... season
Quelle est la date aujourd'hui ?
.... What is the date today?
(C'est) le premier avril

.... (It is) the first of April
Quelle est la date de la fête de ... ?
.... What is the date of the festival of...?
C'est au début/mi/fin février
.... (It's at the) beginning/ middle/end of February
aujourd'hui .... today
après-demain .... the day after tomorrow
demain .... tomorrow
jour (m)............ day
mois (m)........... month

Cooking

assiette (f) .... plate
balance (f) .... scales
beurre (m) *(fondu)* .. (melted) butter
casserole (f) .... pan
couteau (m) .... knife
cuillère (f) .... spoon
farine (f) .... flour
fouet (m) .... whisk
fourchette (f) ...... fork
ingrédients (m) ..... ingredients
papier (m) *sulfurisé* greaseproof paper
pâte (f) *à crêpes* .... batter
petite cuillère (f) .... teaspoon
poêle (f) .... frying pan
saladier (m) .... big bowl/salad bowl
tranche (f) .... slice
ustensiles (m) ...... utensils
verre (m) *à vin* ...... wine glass
verre (m) *gradué* ... measuring jug
ajouter .... to add
casser les œufs ..... to break the eggs
faire fondre .... to melt (something)
faire les crêpes ..... to make (the) pancakes
faire un puits ...... to make a well
laisser reposer ...... to leave to rest
mélanger .... to mix
petit à petit .... little by little
pour chaque personne
.... for each person
verser .... to pour

Festivals and celebrations

Aïd (m) .... Eid
Carnaval (m) .... carnival
Diwali (m)........... Diwali
fête (f) *de la Musique*
.... festival of music
fête (f) *des Rois* ..... festival of the Kings
fête (f) *du muguet* ... festival of the lily of the valley
fête (f) *du printemps* spring festival
Fête (f) *Nationale* ... Bastille Day/National Day
Hanoucca (m)....... Hanukkah
Mardi Gras (m) ..... Mardi Gras ('Fat Tuesday')
Noël (m) .... Christmas
nouvel an (m) *(chinois)*
.... (Chinese) New Year
Pâques (m) .... Easter
anniversaire (m) ..... birthday
fêter .... to celebrate
fête (f) *(religieuse/culturelle)*
.... (religious/cultural) festival
jours (m) *fériés* ..... (bank) holidays

Festival crafts

argent .... silver
bleu .... blue
doré .... golden
vert .... green
carton (m) .... card
ciseaux (m) .... scissors
colle (f) .... glue

écailles (f) .... (fish) scales
feutres (m) .... felt-tip pens
ficelle (f) .... length of string
gommettes (f) ...... gummed paper shapes
argile (f) .... Provençal clay
ligne (f) *(verticale/diagonale)*
.... (vertical/diagonal) line
papier (m) .... paper
scotch (m) *(à double face)*
.... (double-sided) sellotape
velcro (m) .... Velcro®
Vous allez/nous allons ...
.... You are/we are going to ...
dessiner .... to draw
modeler .... to model
peindre .... to paint
photographier .... photograph
poser .... to put
tracer .... to draw (a line)

Festival traditions

bal (m) .... dance
chasse (f) *à l'œuf* ... Easter egg hunt
couronne (f) .... crown
crèche (f) *traditionelle*
.... nativity crib/scene
défilé (m) .... parade
drapeau (m) *Tricolore*
.... (French Tricolore) flag
feu (m) *d'artifice* .... firework; firework display
fève (f) .... charm (hidden in cake for *la fête des Rois*)
horoscope (m)/*zodiac* (m) *chinois*
.... Chinese horoscope
la Marseillaise ...... the *Marseillaise* (French national anthem)
lanterne (f) *chinoise* . Chinese lantern
muguet (m) .... lily of the valley
œuf (m) *de Pâques* .. Easter egg
santon (m).......... traditional miniature clay crèche figure from Provence
solstice (m) .... midsummer day
cachez l'œuf .... hide the egg
Il y a beaucoup de gens
.... There are a lot of people
Qu'est-ce qu'on fête ? What are they, we celebrating?
On fête l'ail ! .... They're/we're celebrating garlic!
Nous mangeons un gâteau spécial
.... We eat a special cake
Le gâteau s'appelle la galette des Rois
.... The cake is called a *galette des Rois*
C'est délicieux ...... It's delicious
Les parents boivent du champagne
.... The parents drink champagne
Les enfants boivent un tout petit peu
.... The children drink a very small amount
Il faut trouver la fève. You have to find the *fève*
Il faut finir la galette . You have to finish the cake

Food and drink

ail (m) .... garlic
beurre (m) .... butter
bol (m) .... bowl
bonbon (m) .... sweet
carotte (f) .... carrot
chocolat (m) .... chocolate
citron (m) .... lemon
confiture (f) .... jam
crêpe (f) .... crêpe/pancake
lait (m) .... milk

mendiant (m) .... a type of sweet; literally 'a beggar'
mirabelle (f) .... plum
œuf (m) .... egg
sel (m) .... salt
sucre (m) .... sugar
table (f) .... table
tomate (f) .... tomato
Bon appétit ! .... Eat well/enjoy your meal

Geography, direction and location
l'Algérie .... Algeria
l'île Maurice .... Mauritius
la Côte d'Ivoire ...... Ivory Coast
la Tunisie .... Tunisia
le Cameroun .... Cameroon
le Mali .... Mali
le Maroc .... Morocco
le Sénégal .... Senegal
la Provence .... Provence
nord (m) .... north
sud (m) .... south
est (m) .... east
ouest (m) .... west
arrondissement (m) . district (of a city)
monde (m) .... the world
pays (m) .... country
place (f) .... the place (note this means 'position' and also 'square' in a town)
rue (f) .... road/street
sentier (m) .... path
au milieu de .... in the middle of
droit .... straight on
droite .... right
en bas .... at the bottom
en haut .... high up
gauche .... left
Où est ...? .... Where is...?
Tournez à gauche/à droite .... Turn left/right
Allez tout droit .... Go straight on
Prenez la première (rue) à droite .... Take the first (road) on the right
Prenez un pas à gauche .... Take one step to the left

Greetings and expressions
Aïd Mubarak ! .... Eid Mubarak! (Happy Eid!)
Bonne année ! (chinoise) .... Happy (Chinese) New Year!
Bonne chance ! ...... Good luck!
Bonne fête ! .... Enjoy the festival!
Joyeux/Bon anniversaire ! .... Happy birthday!
Liberté, Égalité, Fraternité .... Liberty, Equality, Fraternity (French national motto)
Vive la France ! ...... Long live France!
Poisson d'avril ! ...... 'April fish'; phrase said when children are 'got' by the fish on their back
Vive le roi/la reine ! .. Long live the king/queen!

Historical events
l'abolition de l'esclavage .... the abolition of slavery
la révolution (f) ...... the (French) Revolution

Music and dance
basson (m) .... bassoon
batterie (f) .... drum kit
castagnettes (f) .... castanets
chanteur (m) .... singer (m)
chanteuse (f) .... singer (f)

chœur (m) *d'enfants* . children's choir
clarinette (f) .... clarinet
clavier (m) .... keyboard
contrebasse (f) .... double bass
cor (m) .... horn
cymbales (f) .... cymbals
flûte (f) .... flute
flûte à bec (f) ...... recorder
glockenspiel (m) .... glockenspiel
guitare (f) (*électrique*) .... (electric) guitar
hautbois (m) .... oboe
instrument (m) ...... instrument
maracas (m) .... maracas
marimba (m) .... marimba
orchestre (m) ...... orchestra
piano (m) .... piano
saxophone (m) ..... saxophone
tambour (m) .... drum
tambourin (m) ..... tambourine
trombone (m) ..... trombone
trompette (f) ...... trumpet
violon (m) .... violin
violoncelle (m) ...... cello
voix (f) .... voice
xylophone (m) ..... xylophone
Bienvenue à notre concert ! .... Welcome to our concert!
entrée gratuite ...... entrance free
je chante/nous chantons ... . I/we sing...
je danse/nous dansons ... . I/we dance...
je joue du/de la/des ... . I play the ...
je vais/nous allons chanter ... . I am/we are going to sing...

Numbers
un 1
deux 2
trois 3
quatre 4
cinq 5
six 6
sept 7
huit 8
neuf 9
dix 10
onze 11
douze 12
treize 13
quatorze 14
quinze 15
seize 16
dix-sept 17
dix-huit 18
dix-neuf 19
vingt 20
vingt et un 21
vingt-deux 22
vingt-trois 23
vingt-quatre 24
vingt-cinq 25
vingt-six 26
vingt-sept 27
vingt-huit 28
vingt-neuf 29
trente 30
trente et un 31
premier/première ... first
deuxième .... second
troisième .... third
quatrième .... fourth
cinquième .... fifth
sixième .... sixth

septième .... seventh
huitième .... eighth

Religious buildings
balcon (m) .... balcony
bulbe (m) .... onion dome
dôme (m) .... dome
fenêtre (f) .... window
minaret (m) .... minaret
mosquée (f) .... mosque
temple (m) .... temple

Religious figures, artefacts and symbols
Jésus .... Jesus
Joseph .... Joseph
Marie .... Mary
berger (m) .... shepherd
bougie (f) .... candle
Chamach (m) .... shamash (servant candle)
croix (f) .... cross
flamme (f) .... flame
lumière (f) .... light
Ménorah (f) .... menorah
ombre (f) .... shadow
Rois (m) *mages* ..... the (three) Kings

Sentence building
Qu'est-ce que c'est ? . What is it?
C'est un/une ... . It's a...
C'est qui ? .... Who is it?
C'est ... . It's...
Il y a ... . There is...
après .... after
aussi .... also
d'abord .... first of all
dans .... in
dernier/dernière ..... last
derrière .... behind
devant .... in front of
ensuite .... next/after that
finalement .... lastly
là .... there
parce que .... because
puis .... then
sous .... under
sur .... on
voici .... here is
voilà ! .... there it is!

Shapes
carré (m) .... square
cercle (m) .... circle
losange (m) .... diamond
ovale (m) .... oval
rectangle (m) ...... rectangle
triangle (m) .... triangle

Weather
Quel temps fait-il aujourd'hui ? .... What is the weather like today?
Il fait beau .... It is fine
Il fait chaud .... It is hot
Il fait du brouillard ... It is foggy
Il fait du vent .... It is windy
Il fait froid .... It is cold
Il fait mauvais ...... It is bad weather
Il fait 20/moins deux degrés .... It is 20/minus two degrees
Il neige .... It is snowing
Il gèle .... It is freezing
Il pleut .... It is raining
Il y a des nuages ... It is cloudy
Il y a du soleil .... It is sunny

SCHOLASTIC

Also available in this series:

ISBN 978-1407-10203-0

ISBN 978-1407-10207-8

ISBN 978-1407-10208-5

ISBN 978-1407-10206-1

ISBN 978-1407-10205-4

ISBN 978-1407-10204-7

To find out more, call: 0845 603 9091
or visit our website www.scholastic.co.uk